Jack Daniels'
Great Italian Adventure

Jack Daniels' Great Italian Adventure

A Tale About a Dog;
A Six-month Travelogue;
and Stories of Close Encounters with Italy's Bureaucracy

— § —

Dan Houlihan

Book cover designed by Michael Ware
Lavencyon, LLC., Maidens, Virginia
michael@mwarestudio.com

Book edited by Jennifer Cox Houlihan
Faith Canvas, LLC., Fayetteville, Georgia
Facebook.com/JenniferHoulihanTriumphant

Jack Daniels' Great Italian Adventure

ISBN: 978-0-578-55309-2

Printed by Amazon through Kindle Direct Publishing (KDP).

DEDICATION

To our Labrador Retriever, Jack Daniels, and his doggie friends all over the world.

You enrich our lives by just being who you are.

You unconditionally accept us for who we are, warts and all.

You are excited to see us, even if we are gone for only a short time.

You are ready to go on any and every adventure we dream up.

You make us the center of your existence.

Yet, you are totally dependent on us for your every need.

You listen to all our ramblings as if you understand every word.

You melt our stress and warm our hearts.

Jack Daniels patiently waiting for his human mother to exit the Conad grocery store in Perugia, Umbria, Italy.

For A Good Cause

Your purchase of this book will help the following charities.

— § —

The Cliffs Residents Outreach (CRO)

> A 100% volunteer organization, its mission is focused on literacy, nutrition, and mentoring of children of the Upstate Region of South Carolina in order to promote opportunities for lifelong learning. The CRO is a 501(c)(3) non-profit organization that has raised over $3.5 million in the last ten years for children of the Upstate.

— § —

The Choroideremia Research Foundation, Inc. (CRF)

> The Choroideremia Research Foundation is an international, non-profit organization dedicated to raising funds to find a treatment or cure for Choroideremia, a rare inherited retinal degenerative disease that causes blindness. The CRF's mission is to support scientific research, educate those affected by the disease, and inform the general public.

— § —

Each charity above will receive 20% of the annual net profits generated from the sale of this book.

TABLE OF CONTENTS

Introduction   xiii

Chapter One   Six Mile, SC to Verona, Italy via Munich, Germany   1
Chapter Two   Villa Nuba Apartments, Here We Come   9
Chapter Three   Hold the Salt – All About Jack – Pergola Bella   15
Chapter Four   All Things Perugia and a Few Things Greece   21
Chapter Five   Thessaloniki   27
Chapter Six   Castiglione del Lago – Montepulciano – Montalcino   33
Chapter Seven   A Rash Decision and Our First Bureaucratic Encounter   41
Chapter Eight   Spello – Parco Cinofilo – Assisi   47
Chapter Nine   Cortona – Bureaucracy, Round Two   51
Chapter Ten   Bologna   57
Chapter Eleven   To Munich and Back   63
Chapter Twelve   The Bureaucracy Strikes Again and Again and Again   69
Chapter Thirteen   Spoleto and Assisi   75
Pictures   Part I   81
Chapter Fourteen   The Dave Factor   95
Chapter Fifteen   The Dave Factor, Part II; The Bureaucracy Strikes Again 101
Chapter Sixteen   Polizia Nazionale   107
Chapter Seventeen   "In Dublin's Fair City…"   113
Chapter Eighteen   Verona – Pescara   119
Chapter Nineteen   The Ladies of Polizia Nazionale   127
Chapter Twenty   Norcia – Venice – Marostica – Milan   129
Chapter Twenty-One   Residency – Maurizio – Norcia – Montalcino – Gubbio   137
Chapter Twenty-Two   Rome – Muro Lucano – Potenza – Sorrento   143
Pictures   Part II   151
Chapter Twenty-Three   Final Thoughts   163

Acknowledgments   167

About the Author and About the Editor   169

INTRODUCTION

My name is Jack Daniels, and I am a silver Labrador Retriever. There is no apostrophe in my name so as not to be confused with Jack Daniel's, the Tennessee sour-mash whiskey. But since my human owner drinks Jack Daniel's, I suspect my name might have something to do with his favorite drink. I guess it could be worse. He could have named me Old Number 7.

I had hoped that my human parents would be a two-income family with several kids in middle school. That way, they would be so absorbed in their own lives that I could do my thing without too much supervision. Unfortunately, both my human parents are retired with nothing but time on their hands. They constantly watch me like a hawk. I can't get away with anything.

As an example, my human mother has so many, many shoes, I thought that chewing on a shoe every now and then wouldn't be a problem. Boy was I wrong. When they are not looking, I have to settle for stealing socks from the hamper and tissues from the trash can, and then look totally innocent when caught.

My human father, a retired U.S. Army lieutenant colonel, just happens to be the great uncle of my breeder. This explains how I ended up in the Houlihan family. When my human parents saw my pictures on Facebook with my siblings, I must have melted their hearts because they drove all the way to Omaha, NE, to pick me up. It took me a while to get used to them, but I think I have them figured out now. Wrapped around my paw is probably a better description.

I was born on December 25, 2016. You would think I would get special treats and special treatment on Christmas Day, but for me the day brings nothing out of the ordinary. There are more people around our house who make a lot of noise. It seems to me that they get a lot of treats, and other than a few extra pats on the head, I get little more than my two daily feedings of the same boring dog food.

My human mother, Kathy, grew up in a military household, so she traveled a substantial amount with her family. Because my human father, Dan, was in the military, he moved to a new post every three years or so. As a married couple, they continued to travel extensively. When they brought me into their lives, they were supposed to be done with travel so they could focus on me.

Not the case. For some reason, a few months after I arrived, they started planning a six-month adventure to Italy and decided to drag me along. None of us knew what we were getting into. I want to go on record as saying I had no choice in the matter or part in the planning.

As I understand it, other than the obvious things like sightseeing, eating pasta and pizza, and drinking wine, those things that humans seem to enjoy, the main purpose of the trip to Italy was to document Kathy's Italian ancestry. Her grandfather (her mother's father) was born in Italy, as was his father and mother. Her great grandfather and grandmother, on the side of her mother's mother, were also born in Italy. With the right ancestry documentation, a key motivation for the trip, Kathy would be able to apply for dual citizenship with Italy.

Apparently, staying in Italy for six months is not without its challenges. My human father is from Mountmellick, Ireland and emigrated to the United States when he was 11 years old. He has dual citizenship with Ireland and the United States, and has a valid Irish/European Union passport. This allows him to stay in the European Union for as long as he wishes, which is a good thing because U.S. citizens are not allowed to stay longer than 90 days, if visiting the EU as tourists.

My human mother, on the other hand, only has a U.S. passport. But apparently, because she is married to a European Union passport holder, she can stay in the EU beyond 90 days, if accompanied by the EU passport holder. All she has to do is simply apply for a "residency card" after arrival in Italy, at least that is what the Italian Consulate in Coral Gables, Florida told them.

So, there you have it. And I am exhausted. Typing on a keyboard with these big paws is hard work. Good thing there is spell check. Anyway, I am going to turn over the telling of the rest of the story to my human father, who even though he is "retired," still has the energy to play with me and take me on really long walks. All things considered, he takes pretty good care of me, and my human mother spoils me, but that can be our little secret.

Hope you enjoy my story. It is supposed to be my story, but I think this story is going to be all about them.

Jack Daniels

CHAPTER ONE

SIX MILE, SC TO VERONA, ITALY VIA MUNICH, GERMANY

TUESDAY APRIL 24 TO MONDAY APRIL 30

One day, nothing seemed to be going particularly smoothly for my wife. The complex audio-video system in our house was acting up, so all of Kathy's favorite shows failed to get recorded. She made a trip to the grocery, and one of the bags ripped as she made her way to the car. Groceries rolled all over the parking lot. When she returned from the store, delayed due to a traffic accident on our two-lane access road, she learned that one of the key ingredients she needed for the evening's meal was missing. She went to the laundry room to put the wash in the dryer only to find that she failed to start the washer. On the way from the laundry room she tripped over one of Jack's chew toys. I heard a scream and as she blew past my office, she muttered something like, "I can't take this anymore. I want the simple life. I am moving to Italy."

She wasn't all that clear as she slammed the door to the bedroom. Was *she* moving to Italy or were *we* moving to Italy? As I sat in my office, I carefully examined my options, none of which seemed particularly attractive. Say nothing and be perceived as insensitive? Try and console but blurt out something stupid that further exacerbates the situation? Being the coward that I am, I elected to let time pass and see who would emerge from the bedroom.

From his position on the couch, Jack can see into my office, and having observed the recent series of events, he seemed to approve the option I selected. For the next few hours, the bedroom door remained closed, but I started to receive nonstop emails with links to homes for sale throughout Italy. I took that as a sign that I might be included in the relocation planning. In typical John McEnroe fashion, I thought to myself, "She can't be serious, can she? Why Italy? Why not Ireland?"

Kathy's father, William Nelson, was of Irish-Scotch-Welsh-German heritage. Her mother, Leonilda (Linda) Ianniccari, was Italian through and through, and Kathy is all about her mother. Kathy's four siblings are more ethnically balanced or perhaps favor their father's looks. Kathy has beautiful dark brown eyes and when her hair is cut short, she is the spitting image of her mother. And, like her mother, she is a little on the fiery side.

Kathy loves to cook, as did her mother, and growing up in the Nelson household, Sunday was always pasta and gravy day, an event that involved the entire family. Now when Kathy makes gravy, regardless of the day of the week, we always say, "It's starting to smell like Sunday." There is not a cooking show that she misses, and her list of recipes is legendary. Not only does Kathy like to cook, she loves to entertain. The bigger the spread she lays out, the happier she becomes. When compliments come her way, she brushes them aside with, "Thanks, but I am just a good recipe reader."

Her love of cooking is matched by her quick wit and sense of humor. She can find humor in any situation, perhaps not on this particular day, and I am always amazed by the funny stories she is able to tell about an occasion we both experienced. As she regales others with a side-splitting recount of the event we attended, I think to myself, "Where was I when all this was going on?"

Marriage is all about compromise, at least I keep telling myself that, and when the dust settled a few hours later, I proposed a six-month stay in either Italy or in Ireland in lieu of moving to either place. Try before you buy was my self-serving philosophy. If we totally loved the experience, we could consider moving permanently. Who would have thought that she would agree to such a silly idea? But she did. And she chose Italy over Ireland. What now, Danny Boy? The simple answer: research, plan, and, somehow, make it happen.

During the solar eclipse of 2017, we were with Dave and Joan, our good friends from our Cliffs at Keowee Springs neighborhood in South Carolina, sipping wine and watching the celestial drama unfold. We shared our plans and our dilemma about deciding where to set up our base of operations in Italy. "That's easy," said Dave. "Stay with Giuseppe in Perugia." Dave and Joan had stayed with Giuseppe Nuzzaci at his Villa Nuba Apartments in Perugia, Italy several years earlier, and they thought that Perugia's central location would be ideal for our needs.

A call to Giuseppe the next day, during which he waxed eloquent about Dave and Joan, allowed us to secure a two-bedroom apartment for the period of May 1 through October 31. Over the next few days, we successfully wired a Euro deposit to Giuseppe to lock in our accommodations. With that accomplished, we now turned our attention to the issue of transporting Jack Daniels to Italy.

Preparing to ship a dog from the United States to the European Union is a daunting task. After extensive research on the subject, I developed a feeling similar to the one I get when a new prescription medicine arrives at my house. By the time I read the multi-page warning that comes with the prescription medicine about all the possible dangerous side-effects of taking the medicine, I wonder if taking it is worth the trouble.

Early on, we learned some good news about taking Jack with us to Europe. Neither Germany nor Italy, the two countries we would be visiting with Jack, require a quarantine period. What they do require, however, among other things, is an authenticated International Pet Travel Certificate.

While we have a wonderful veterinarian in Dr. Chris Burton at Pickens Animal Hospital, he is not authorized to issue an International Pet Travel Certificate, so we had to get a referral to a doctor so authorized. We were referred to a doctor at Powdersville Animal Hospital, about a 25-minute drive from our house.

The next thing we discovered is that actions related to transporting a dog to Europe must take place in a specific sequence. From the day your plane lands in the EU, you count back 10 days and, within that window, the doctor must perform his final exam and sign all the travel documents. The main purpose of the final exam is to see if there was any adverse reaction to the rabies vaccination previously administered to the pet. But to determine that, you need to wait 21 days after the vaccination injection before the final exam can be completed.

Within that same 10-day time window, the signed paperwork must then be mailed or taken to the nearest Department of Agriculture office for review and approval. Not wanting to take any chances with the U.S. Postal Service, I drove to Columbia, South Carolina, and walked the paperwork through the Department of Agriculture.

In addition to the rabies vaccination, the EU requires that an ISO Certified 15-digit microchip be embedded between the dog's shoulder blades, and the microchip must be implanted before the rabies vaccine is administered. Based on all our research, we elected to go with the Datamars Ultra Slim Microfinder microchip, which was available through The Pet Travel Store. Neither the insertion of the microchip nor the rabies shot seemed to bother Jack Daniels in the slightest.

However, before these two events could take place, the doctor needs to perform a complete health examination, make sure all other shots are up to date, and then start the paperwork process. That initial travel exam cannot take place more than 60 days before travel begins. A lot had to happen within 60 days of takeoff. As you might suspect, there were fees associated with each step in this exhausting process.

Since our boy Jack weighs more than 70 pounds, he is required to travel in the cargo hold of the plane, and not all planes are outfitted to carry live animals.

Therefore, early in the process we had to determine which airline to use, and we elected to go with Lufthansa for several reasons.

We found that Lufthansa had the best reputation among the major air carriers for live pet transport. We also found that Lufthansa allowed us to book our own tickets and Jack's ticket at the same time. American Airlines, as an example, would allow us to book our tickets, but Jack's ticket could not be booked until 10 days before the flight departed. No matter how good the odds were that Jack would make the flight, and despite the multiple assurances we received from American Airlines to that fact, we were not going to take a chance that Jack would not be on the same plane.

Our closest airport is Greenville, SC, and you cannot get to Europe from Greenville without one or more stops. That left us two options: flying from Atlanta, GA or flying from Charlotte, NC. Since Lufthansa had a pet friendly plane direct from Charlotte to Munich, Germany, we chose to go with Lufthansa.

The final piece of the puzzle was to get an airline-approved travel crate for our boy. Since the requirements are that the dog must be able to stand in the crate and have a certain amount of head clearance, and be able to turn around inside the crate with ease, we purchased an extra-large Sky Kennel crate, mattress, and bowls from the Pet Travel Store.

Our travel strategy for Jack was to make sure he was "dog tired" when he boarded his crate at the Charlotte airport. Having spent three weeks at Upstate Dog Training in Greer for his initial obedience training back in October of 2017, we decided to return him there for the last six days before we boarded the flight. Since Jack is still an undisciplined free spirit, I believe this is called pouring good money after bad.

Boarding Jack for training would give us time to pack without Jack stealing all our socks and underwear from our suitcases, and give Jack time to exhaust himself playing with the other dogs at Upstate Dog Training. On this pre-departure visit, Jack would be in training for three days: playtime on the weekend; then training, playtime, and a bath before we picked him up. By then, we hoped he would be ready to sleep all the way to Germany.

Armed with Jack's authenticated International Pet Travel Certificate and complete medical history, on April 24 we headed to Charlotte, NC. The trip from our house to the Charlotte airport was uneventful, other than needing a driver and a Ford Excursion to haul four 70-pound suitcases (allowed by Lufthansa business class), four carry-on bags (also allowed by Lufthansa), two passengers, a dog, and a very large airline crate.

The initial requirement was that Jack had to be at the Lufthansa ticket counter three hours before the flight's departure time. We were able to negotiate with the ticket agent to get him there an hour and a half before departure. We checked in three hours before the flight and got rid of our luggage, then spent the next hour and a half walking the grassy area at the cell phone parking lot, pleading with Jack to do his business and getting him to swallow Benadryl tablets. By that point, I think Jack thought we had lost our minds.

While killing time at the airport, Kathy noticed gouges and scratches and cuts on Jack's body, which I attributed to rough play time with the other dogs at Upstate Dog Training. We also noticed the start of a rash on his belly and tiny bumps along his back. It was go time for the flight, though, so there was nothing we could do about it then.

After all the pre-planning, and all the coordination phone calls, and all the veterinary appointments for Jack, and having the Department of Agriculture approve and seal all the papers for his travel to the EU, no one, and I mean no one, in Charlotte even asked for, let alone looked at, his travel paperwork.

The Lufthansa ticket agent took my $400 crate fee, called a customs inspector who examined the crate to make sure we were not shipping anything more than a dog, then put some stickers on Jack's crate, and wished us a good flight. Maybe the paperwork gets scrutinized on the other side of the pond? Even before takeoff, our boy Jack was into my wallet for nearly $1,400. But then, as Jack mentioned in the introduction, he had no part in the planning process, so it's all on us.

Kathy and I enjoyed the flight, other than being nervous about our dog down in the cargo hold, but that feeling subsided the more wine we consumed. After we glided through passport control at the Munich airport and headed to baggage claim, Jack and his crate, unsoiled by him after being imprisoned within for 11 hours, arrived around the same time as our luggage. We got two luggage carts, removed Jack from his crate, filled the crate with our carry-on bags, retrieved our four suitcases, and pushed our way out through the "nothing to declare door" into the middle of terminal 2 at the Munich airport, passing by all those limo drivers holding up name plates.

It felt like we had just done something totally illegal. Best I can guess, the ticket clerk in Charlotte, two baggage handlers in Charlotte, and two baggage handlers in Munich, were the only ones (other than our friends), who knew that Jack Daniels was in Europe.

Kathy waited with our luggage carts just inside the exit of terminal 2, while Jack and I set out on a mission to deposit his pent up bodily fluids. I got some strange looks when I asked several people the question, "Where can I find some grass?" Nicht fur me, fur mein hund! Through the massive open-air courtyard between terminal 2 and terminal 1, through terminal 1, and finally, at least 400 yards later, we made it out to a loading dock that had a piece of grass the size of a small apartment. The relieved look on Jack's face was priceless.

To get over jet lag, catch our breath, and get Jack acclimated to Europe, we stayed at the Hilton Munich Airport for a few days. The Hilton, which is attached to the terminal, was truly excellent. Germans love their dogs, and Jack was allowed, even welcomed, into the hotel's restaurants. At each meal, Jack got his bowl of water before we were asked what we wanted to drink.

The next day, I picked up our "straight from the factory brand new" Citroen C4 Picasso minivan. Leasing a car for six months has significant cost advantages over renting a car for the same period. French companies lease new cars to European visitors and then, weeks or months later, sell the vehicles as "used" to folks wanting to avoid the onerous Value-Added Tax that France imposes on the sale of new cars.

Thanks to an amazing GPS system in the Citroen, I was able to navigate into the heart of Munich and drop off the airline crate with our good German friend, David Eckart. The next day, after a superb multi-station breakfast buffet, like the kind one finds in large hotels all over Europe, we crammed our eight bags and dog into the Citroen and headed to the Hilton Munich Park hotel for a few additional days of enjoying beer and schnitzel with David, his wife Connie, and David's mother, Helga.

Friday night, we all met at the Menterschwaige Restaurant and Beer Garden just south and east of the city center (it is as refined a beer garden as large beer gardens go). Saturday, we dined alone at an Italian restaurant within walking distance of our hotel (prepping for our journey to Italy on Monday). And Sunday afternoon we met our friends at another beer garden, the Chinesischer Turm Restaurant and Beer Garden (huge and not so refined, but still very enjoyable) in the middle of the English Garden Park just behind our hotel.

On Monday, well rested and raring to go, we drove from Munich to Garmisch-Partenkirchen, one of our favorite small villages in all the world, to top off the gas tank in our Citroen. We also bought an Austrian highway toll ticket before heading through Austria to a half-way point just on the north side of Verona in a small village of San Pietro in Cariano, Verona.

The place where we stayed, Hotel Villa Giona, was serendipitous in every sense. I had made a reservation at a hotel near the center of Verona, but when I emailed them the night before our arrival to confirm we were travelling with a dog, they informed me that they no longer accept pets. I cancelled that hotel on Expedia and booked another – a complete shot in the dark.

Our shot in the dark, the Hotel Villa Giona, was amazing. The hotel is the former residence of the family that owned hundreds of acres of surrounding vineyards for hundreds of years. In the 1990s, the property was renovated and converted into a boutique hotel that now accommodates just 18 guest rooms. It has palatial grounds that are surrounded by vineyards. The hotel's website is worth checking out: www.villagiona.it.

We ate at Villa Giona, which had a really limited menu, and enjoyed a great bottle of 2014 Cantina Paolo Cottini, Valpolicella Ripasso for the exorbitant sum of 22 Euro. The wine would probably cost 10-12 Euro in a grocery store.

While we were settling into our two-level guest apartment, Jack, as he likes to do, decided he needed to explore his new surroundings on the lower level of our suite. Somehow, Jack tripped over some wires behind a round table in the corner of the room and forced the lamp on the table to slide off the table, bounce off the wall and then bounce back onto the table, shattering the table's glass top.

I believed it was the right thing for me to let the hotel know about his misdeed. So, upon checking out, I explained that our family had experienced some uncoordinated actions near the tabletop glass. The desk clerk got the manager, to whom I repeated our story about the broken table. The manager was not amused, and started mumbling about monetary restitution and the need to call his boss, which he did.

So here we have the "manager" of this four-star boutique hotel who is so worried about an 18-inch round, cheap, glass table top, that he feels it necessary to call his off-site "upper manager" for guidance. Whatever happened to organizations delegating decisions to the lowest level possible? His "upper manager" wanted 65 Euro for what I deemed was about an eight Euro glass top. I mentioned the concept of fair wear and tear, and the fact that the hotel carries property insurance. After a suitable amount of hand gesturing and negotiation, we reached an accommodation. While the hotel stay was most enjoyable, I was not remorseful when I bid the manager Grazie and Arrivederci.

CHAPTER TWO

VILLA NUBA APARTMENTS, HERE WE COME

TUESDAY, MAY 1 TO SUNDAY, MAY 6

The drive from Hotel Villa Giona to our final destination and home base, the Villa Nuba Apartments in Perugia, Umbria was without adventure, for the most part. May 1 is a holiday in Italy, and, thankfully, the vast majority of the traffic was heading in the opposite direction.

For our side, the ride along the A22 Autostrada was a breeze. We clipped along at 120 to 130 KPH (62-78 MPH) in the slow lane, and were being passed on the left as if we were standing still. For the other side, not so much: we witnessed at least a dozen traffic jams spanning miles in length, which were interspersed with periods of slow moving traffic. The canine gods were smiling on us.

We took a break at an Autostrada rest stop, and, since the car was at half full, I decided to fill up. The cost was 50 Euro for half a tank, which equates to $120 for a full tank. Ahia. (Italian for Ouch.) Past Modena, past Bologna, past Florence, we exited the Autostrada toll booth and merged onto the E45/RA6 towards Rome and then diverted towards Perugia. During this part of the trip, we crossed 100 valleys, so we were either in a mountain tunnel or on a seriously elevated highway. The scenery was stunning; when not in the tunnels, of course.

While the quality of the Autostrada was amazing, the E45 highway could have been a testing ground for tanks. Since traffic was light, I was able to weave around the uneven and pot-holed parts of the road, large spans of which were under rehabilitation, all the while keeping an eye on the rear-view mirror for those bent on imbedding themselves in the Citroen's exhaust pipe.

Finally, we parked at Via Eugubina 69, Perugia. No sign anywhere of Via Eugubina 70, the street address of Villa Nuba. As it turns out, Via Eugubina 70 is nowhere near Via Eugubina 69; and by nowhere near I mean from Via Eugubina 69 you drive down the street for two blocks, into the roundabout, right, then straight for three more blocks, left on a gravel road, and then up the hill for another two blocks along a road where all the houses are numbered 70.

Giuseppe Nuzzaci, our host, met us at Via Eugubina 69 and guided us to Villa Nuba. Villa Nuba is comprised of the main house where Giuseppe and his parents live, and three apartments: two two-bedroom apartments and one one-bedroom apartment.

When I first called Giuseppe after we stopped at Via Eugubina 69, he said he would be there in 15 minutes. I was thinking 15 U.S. minutes. Maybe even 15 Italian minutes. But not 15 Nuzzaci minutes. Thirty-five minutes later, up shows Giuseppe. By then, Jack was at the end of his leash, and Kathy was not too far behind.

Recently separated, Giuseppe has a five-year-old son, Lorenzo, whom he gets to see on a weekly basis. Giuseppe is about 5'10" and thin, maybe 160 pounds; close-cropped black hair with sprinkles of gray; his hairline receding in two spots, one above each eye. I would put Giuseppe in his early 40s, but he is a smoker, so he may actually be younger than he looks. Giuseppe has a New York or New Jersey style about him: assertive, talkative, in your "space" kind of guy, but not offensively so. Like many Italians, he speaks with his hands, and must have touched us 30 times during our initial 10-minute conversation.

Dave and Joan, our eclipse-watching friends, recommended Villa Nuba to us after having stayed there for two weeks in 2015. Their reviews were glowing. Not sure that Kathy will ever forgive them for their recommendation or forgive me for making the booking. A picture is worth a thousand words, and we looked at every picture on the Villa Nuba website and read every word. So how did we miss the fact that a fully equipped kitchen at Villa Nuba did not include an oven? A dishwasher, yes, but an oven, no. When we entered the kitchen in our apartment, the look on Kathy's face was the exact opposite of the look on Jack's face when we found that patch of grass at the Munich airport.

How do you fix eggplant parmigiana without an oven? If you are staying for just one week, then who needs an oven? For two weeks, with a lot of rainy days, there is a chance you may use an oven. Six months without an oven could make a budding chef borderline suicidal. Better make that homicidal. And apparently it did. With Lorena (I'll sever your reproductive appendage) Bobbitt-Houlihan next to me, I began sleeping with one eye open. On the bright side, early on at Villa Nuba we discovered that all the kitchen knives were really dull, so my survival chances were looking up.

— § —

Villa Nuba is situated among other large villas on a very hilly section of land. Other than the gravel road going in and out and the foundations on which the villas are built, the rest of the land is quite steep, with gates and fencing everywhere. We were hoping for rolling hills where Jack could roam untethered in every sense; a canine scene from *The Sound of Music*. Not to be, but we coped.

When we checked into one of the Hilton hotels in Germany at the beginning of our trip, the hotel provided a large blanket for Jack's use. The blanket became part of the family. In our home base Villa Nuba apartment, we had a combined dining and living area. The living area had two chairs and a sofa bed. The blanket adorned the sofa bed and that is where Jack would hang out day and night.

During our stay in Munich, Jack's skin bumps had become more pronounced and more plentiful. His appetite had not diminished nor had his energy level, and other than an increase in itching, Jack seemed oblivious to the skin condition. However, by the time we reached Perugia, the condition worsened and our concerns were heightened.

Exit the villa gates and proceed along the winding gravel road, and you reach the city street. Turn right, and you soon come to a gas station, and then a grocery store, and shortly past the grocery is a one-person veterinary clinic run by Dr. Massimo Crecco, with whom Giuseppe had great experience and in whom he had the utmost confidence.

Early Wednesday morning (Tuesday was a holiday), Giuseppe went with me to the clinic to meet Dr. Massimo so I could outline, with Giuseppe's translation help, Jack's condition. We left having an appointment for later that same morning.

For whatever reason, Jack loves to go to veterinary clinics. It must be the smell of other dogs. You would think he would know better. At six months, he was sedated to have his "cherry eye" repaired. At seven months, he was sedated so he could have x-rays for a severe limp in one of his front legs. At 10 months, he was sedated for his neuter surgery. Yet here he comes, happy to see everyone at every clinic he visits, and his visit to the clinic in Perugia was no exception.

Previous calls to Upstate Dog Training and to Dr. Burton in South Carolina led us to believe that Jack's rash was due to the shampoo the dog-training site used. Now it was up to our Italian veterinarian. A quick exam, then the old quarter-inch wide thermometer up the backside for more than a minute, and, finally, the doctor cut open and scraped the contents of one of Jack's bumps onto a glass slide so he could examine it under a microscope.

Dr. Massimo advised that the rash was not caused by a parasite of any kind. He thought it might be some sort of contact dermatitis that should be easily treatable with antibiotics and a medicated shampoo. Dr. Massimo did a blood draw, gave Jack two shots and gave me a prescription for antibiotics. The doctor's efforts were worth 50 Euro, which was comparable to what I pay in the States for an office visit. The antibiotics, on the other hand, cost 135 Euro. We headed back to Villa Nuba and followed the doctor's orders.

— § —

Overall, the weather during our entire six months in Italy was a wonderful surprise. The first two weeks in May were quite rainy, very uncharacteristic for that time of year according to Giuseppe. But after that, the weather was absolutely delightful. The biggest and most unexpected bonus was that, even in the month of August, we experienced little to no humidity and, as a result, never turned on the air conditioner in our apartment. The weather in September and October was equally spectacular.

As I said, though, the weather our first week in Perugia was not all that great. After three days of overcast and cold conditions with intermittent rain, none of which did anything to improve Lorena Bobbitt-Houlihan's disposition, I texted Giuseppe for a good local restaurant that was not in the old city, and that would have plenty of parking so we would not have to walk too much. He recommended Ristorante Il Pettirosso because of the food, the price, and the amazing view. But Giuseppe – have you not noticed that it's raining?

To reach Il Pettirosso, we did not have to drive into the old city, but we did have to drive all the way around Perugia to the opposite side of the city and then up a single lane mountain road to the top of a hill located half way between Perugia and Lake Trasimeno. No menu. You eat what the chef cooked that day: an antipasto, a pasta dish, a meat dish, dessert and a jug of "vino rosso della casa." It was a 55-minute drive, and we just made the deadline for lunch, but the sun did come out as we were finishing up, and the view was indeed amazing. Funny what the sun does for one's disposition.

Friday, we were back at the veterinary clinic for more tests. Jack received a shot of cortisone because his condition had not improved. It had even worsened. Dr. Massimo thought Jack had an allergic reaction to some thing or things unknown. Saturday, we were back for the test results from the blood draw. Now, we needed cortisone pills to go along with the antibiotics. This latest visit and test cost 135 Euro.

With three clinic visits in four days, I started doing a cost/benefit analysis. Without Jack's acquisition cost, the cost of all his surgeries, his travel fees, and overseas medical costs, I could be well on my way to a deposit on a new Mercedes, and Lorena (where is my oven and what have you done to my dog) Bobbitt-Houlihan would not be plotting her revenge. But then, how do you put a price on canine companionship? In fairness to the costly services of the Dr. Massimo, his wife, Simona, who speaks three or four languages, came in for each of Jack's visits to interpret and explain. It is hard to put a value on excellent service like that. Perhaps the word I am looking for is - priceless?

Our first evening at Villa Nuba had been a bit underwhelming. Since May 1 was a holiday, not much was open. We drove a quarter of the way up the hill towards the old city, parked and then hiked our way up, up, and up to the city center. After an hour of exploring the old city, Kathy popped into a deli and bought some cheese, ham, salami, bread, and wine and we headed back to Villa Nuba for our first "meal."

On Saturday after Jack's appointment, we decided to explore some more. Near Dr. Massimo's office is a pharmacy, and just a few yards past them both is a roundabout. Beyond the roundabout you have a bank, a little later a pizza parlor, followed shortly by a fruit market, and later a coffee and pastry shop. All of the comforts of home are within a short mile of the villa. Since the weather this particular day was rain free, we walked this same route and extended the trek uphill about another mile towards the old city, along which we discovered a plethora of stores, restaurants, pastry and coffee shops.

Back in South Carolina my doctor, David Koontz, is a really great person as well as a great physician. When I told Dr. Koontz we were going to Italy for six months to eat pasta and drink wine, he was not too happy. He told me I'd better walk every day. Not one to ignore my doctor's orders, I walked to the pastry shop every day for my cappuccino and marmalade croissant (cornetto con marmellata).

— § —

Italy is a somewhat socialized economy. Just how socialized was enlightening. Late morning on Wednesday, before Giuseppe and I went to the veterinary clinic, we talked to Giuseppe about how to turn on the heat. He advised us that in all areas of Italy you are not allowed to turn on the heating or air conditioning except during designated times of the year for your locality. The period for using heat had passed, so bundle up if you are cold. I had a very similar experience living in in the Army quarters.

As you drive along the gravel road towards Villa Nuba, just to the right of the villa's entrance gate, you see four large trashcans, each with its own colored lid – green, yellow, blue and black. Every villa has the same four trashcans outside its gate. Inside the tiny kitchen at Villa Nuba are four smaller but similarly color-coded trashcans into which you must recycle everything you use. Room for four kitchen trashcans but not for an oven?

Recycling is not optional in Italy. You must deposit into each can those items that are supposed to be deposited in said can. Failure to do so can result in a 75 Euro fine for the property owner. The recycling system is ultra-complex. Not all paper goes in the paper trashcan, only certain paper. Not all cardboard in the cardboard trashcan, only certain cardboard. Not all plastic, but certain plastic. And thus, it goes. Who needs this kind of stress?

Whenever Jack and I went on long walks and he made a contribution on the street, sidewalk, or grass, I deposited his goodie bag in the nearest available trashcan, hoping I picked the right color, and hoping I was not going to be the cause of the owner receiving a 75 Euro fine.

CHAPTER THREE

HOLD THE SALT — ALL ABOUT JACK — PERGOLA BELLA

MONDAY, MAY 7 TO SATURDAY MAY 12

Growing up in Catholic grade schools and high schools, I always believed that the head of the Catholic Church, the Pope, was kind, holy, saintly, and reverent (I believe in redundancy). In medieval times, apparently, Popes acted more like crime bosses. In 1497, Pope Alexander VI excommunicated Girolamo Savonarola, an Italian Dominican friar from Florence, for continuing to preach concepts with which the Pope disagreed. In 1498, he threatened to excommunicate the entire Province of Florence if Savonarola was not silenced. Now that's what I call collateral damage.

Provinces in Italy feuded all the time for many reasons, mostly religion, meaning power, but not always. Pisa and Florence were at odds over something and Pisa, because of its location on the Mediterranean, cut off all the supply lines of salt to Florence and points east. As a result, in Tuscany and Umbria, which includes our home base Perugia, salt became scarce, and prices skyrocketed.

Then in 1540, Pope Paul III imposed a tax on salt because he wanted everyone to buy their salt from the Papal supplier. A saintly businessman, perhaps? The Umbrians, incensed by the Pope's edict to purchase salt from the pontificate, rebelled and stopped using salt in bread and limited salt consumption everywhere possible. Not necessarily a smart decision, since salt was the country's main avenue for food preservation. Regardless, unsalted Umbrian bread became a badge of courage.

It is now 2018, and the salt tax has been gone for hundreds of years, yet many stores in Umbria sell bread made without salt. Bread without salt has a crust like a brick, interior like a cake, and taste devoid of all flavor. The point of all this? The coffee-pastry-bread shop 600 yards up the road from us, Cerquiglini Café e Patisserie, used salt, and, according to Giuseppe, folks from all around the city go there to buy their bread. Since we had already sampled unsalted bread from the local grocery store, the good news about having salted bread within easy reach was a definite plus for Lorena Bobbitt-Houlihan, just not good enough to offset the absence of an oven.

15

Jack seemed to be progressing nicely from his twice a day antibiotics and his once a day cortisone pills. The bumps on his skin that multiplied on his back and sides and transitioned into blotches on his belly subsided considerably. We hoped to get a clean bill of health when next we saw Dr. Massimo.

After all the restaurants and beer gardens we visited in Germany, Jack became accustomed to dense crowds. He appeared neither to be amused nor bothered by the hundreds of feet he encountered at eye level in every direction. He was getting better behaved in restaurants, but it would still take time for him to explore every inch of the floor around our table before he settled down.

When in Rome, do as Roman dogs do. In South Carolina, it seemed that Jack was not comfortable doing his business unless he was on a patch of plush grass. Since coming to Europe where plush grass is rare, Jack adapted seemingly well to his new environment. Whether on gravel roads, streets, sidewalks or driveways, when the urge hit, Jack responded. Sunday on our walk, with no notice, he darted off the sidewalk to drop a load a few feet in the street. I was nearly decapitated by a bus while I was trying to clean up the environment.

Monday, Jack had a couple of firsts. We went to a small but most sophisticated mall, Centro Commerciale Collestrada, about a 20-minute beautiful drive from Villa Nuba in the general direction of Assisi. The mall had underground parking with escalators up to the mall shops. On the escalators, Jack had a tough time figuring out how he was actually moving while his feet were perfectly still. I tried to explain, but I don't think he was paying too much attention.

Jack was allowed in the mall and in nearly all the shops in the mall; another first. We wandered the mall for a while, but the slick marble floors required too much effort for Jack's paws to navigate safely, so we exited the complex and people-watched while Kathy shopped. It appeared to me that a large number of Italians smoke. For the hour plus we were hanging out at the mall entrance, a significant number of folks, I would say 25 percent, stopped for a while to finish their cigarettes before entering. Just an unscientific observation.

— § —

When we booked the six months at Villa Nuba, we knew that one week had already been pre-booked by another party, the week of May 19 to May 26. Which meant two things. We needed to find somewhere to go for that week, and if we could not take Jack, then we needed to find a good temporary home for him.

As it turned out, Theo and Heather, friends we made on a Danube cruise in 2016, live in Australia but visit Greece for extended periods every year or so. Theo was born on the island of Samos and still has a number of relatives spread around Greece. When we planned this Italy trip, I contacted them about meeting in Greece for the week we needed to be out of our apartment. We agreed to meet in Thessaloniki for five days and renew old acquaintances.

What about a place for Jack? At our request, Giuseppe had done a lot of research and selected two pet pensiones for us to visit. On further review, Giuseppe was convinced that one of the two would best meet our needs. So, on Tuesday off we went, me following Giuseppe through the highly congested streets of Perugia, in and out of a thousand traffic circles to our destination 45 minutes west and south of the city. Not about to get lost, I stayed right on Giuseppe's bumper and in so doing angered a few hundred Perugians with my New York cabbie style of driving.

We arrived at Pergola Bella (Pensione per Cani e Gatti), a large dog retreat out in the countryside and spent time touring the facility with the owner, Loris Testi. Loris' wife and daughters speak several languages, but Loris is "just an Italian," his words as translated by Giuseppe. Giuseppe did a masterful job of interpreting for us and getting all our questions answered. With Jack now having a pensione reservation for the time we would be in Greece, we started to breathe a little easier about leaving him in a foreign country for the first time.

When we met with Loris Testi, he let us know that he needed the name of a veterinarian for emergency purposes, and if we did not have one, then he had one he uses. We mentioned our experience with Massimo, and it turned out Loris knew him and had great respect for him, which was nice to hear.

It was now 12:48 p.m. and my last question to Loris was about recommending a nice place for us to have lunch before returning to Perugia. Not only did he have a place in mind, he called them to make sure they were open, and then volunteered to escort us to the restaurant. Twenty minutes later, on a road in the opposite direction of Perugia, we arrived at Hotel Ristorante Da Elio just outside the town of Piegaro. Loris entered the restaurant with us and introduced us to the owner, then left us to enjoy our lunch.

No agenda, no timetable, no rush to get or be anywhere. This is part of the reason we were six months in Italy. We just wanted to soak up the culture at our own pace as opportunities presented themselves. So here we were, off the beaten path, in an idyllic country setting, at a restaurant that only locals frequent, and seated at a table that was ours for as long as we wanted, all because Jack knew the owner of a pet pensione. Priceless.

In our best Italian, we ordered a bottle of vino rosso della casa and a bottle of still water. Kathy ordered the "tagliata di vitellone rucola e pomodorini" (sliced veal tenderloin with rocket and cherry tomatoes). I ordered the veal tenderloin with black truffle. Our waiter said either they were out of black truffle or that as an American I was not authorized to eat black truffle, so he pointed to the item above. Not having a clue as to what he said, I nodded in the affirmative and off he went.

Our waiter served an appetizer of bread with prosciutto and melted cheese that was absolutely delicious. We both had the "insalata mista" accompanied by an endless supply of bread (the salted kind) and olive oil. Both meals were served with a side of sautéed spinach. In my travels, I have eaten veal, as in schnitzel, but never veal tenderloin. This cut was the size of a rib eye steak but thicker, cooked to perfection, tender, and bursting with flavor.

We followed the meal up with Limonce limoncello, one of the better ones I have consumed, and as it turned out after research, Italy's number one selling limoncello. We followed the limoncello with a couple of café cappuccinos. The question now was who was going to drive back to Perugia. So glad Jack got his driver's license before we left South Carolina.

— § —

It is difficult, if not downright impossible, to know when Lorena is going to appear. She did not show up in Germany, which was a good thing. For the first few rainy days in Perugia, she appeared on a more frequent basis – one might even say hourly. As Jack's condition improved, Lorena's appearances diminished.

The morning we were heading to Pergola Bella we were supposed to meet Giuseppe to discuss some issues with our accommodations (code word – oven). Operating on Nuzzaci time, he showed up 40 minutes late and Lorena was out in full force. Jack and I came up with an excuse to get out of the blast zone. When we retuned, Kathy advised that we would have an oven in our unit when we got back from Greece. Well played, Lorena Bobbitt-Houlihan, well played.

Wednesday afternoon we met with Dr. Massimo, and he was pleased with Jack's progress. He recommended we continue the medication until the supplies were exhausted, and then do a final check-up in one week. Earlier that same day, we found a great pet store, Grifovet Pet Shop, which carried the same brand of dog food Jack uses. So, all things Jack appeared to be trending in the right direction.

— § —

On Saturday, we met with Elisabetta, a guide from the tour organization Umbria With Me, and did a two-hour walking tour of the walled city of Perugia. Elisabetta, who speaks better English than either one of us, did a masterful job of showing us the nooks and crannies of Perugia's city center, in addition to the city's main tourist and historical attractions.

Having recently lost her 16-year-old golden retriever, she was most sympathetic to our decision to bring Jack to Italy. Jack was extremely well behaved for the two-plus hours. Apparently, this particular Saturday was bring-your-dog-to-Perugia day, so Jack had a ball interacting with his Italian cousins.

When our "former" good friends Dave and Joan (the couple that burned us on the apartment oven - pun intended), visited Perugia, they compiled a list of their favorite restaurants, which they provided before our departure. We decided to have lunch at one of their recommendations, Il Cantinone, since the restaurant was close to where we parked. The restaurant is down a quiet street, just off the main piazza in Perugia. After a long morning, Jack appreciated the solitude of a sidewalk table in the shade. We got a liter of vino rosso della casa for eight Euro, I am serious, two "insalata mistas," two delicious pizzas, and two cappuccinos.

After lunch and figuring out how to pay for our parking, we headed home, and the three of us decided to try this Italian siesta thing. We all agreed that it could be habit forming.

CHAPTER FOUR

ALL THINGS PERUGIA AND A FEW THINGS GREECE

SUNDAY, MAY 13 TO SATURDAY MAY 19

It seems to me that an "I" should be an "I" no matter where, when, or how "I" is used. In German, "I" is "Ich": I am hungry – Ich bin hungrig. I am from - Ich komme aus. I would like – Ich mochte.

In Italian, I am hungry is "Ho fame." I would like is "Vorrei." I am from is "Io sono." How in the world am I supposed to survive with this language where an "I" is not always an "I?" And another thing about this language. Words that sound alike and are spelled alike should have generally the same meaning.

In Italian, a bicycle is "bicicletta." And a glass is "bicchiere." Early in my dining adventures here, I ordered a bicycle of the house red wine. The waiter raised both eyebrows, gave a strange smirk, and I am sure he mumbled something derogatory under his breath, but to his credit, he brought me what I was attempting to order.

Jack, on the other hand, did not appear to be bothered by the language. No matter who spoke to him, he smiled, wagged his tail, and bobbed up and down as if he was ready to play whatever game they had in mind. Despite his apparent indifference to the language barrier, he might have been going through somewhat of an identity crisis.

Apparently, silver Labrador Retrievers are quite rare in Italy, so no matter where we were in Perugia, he got a ton of looks and a lot of personal attention. Everywhere we went, people approached and said "bello, bello" or "bello cane." Jack heard this so many times that he began to look at me as if to say, "I thought my name was Jack?"

— § —

So why Perugia, you ask? Simply put, location. We wanted to use wherever we settled as a base of operations for exploring Italy. Perugia is half way between the Mediterranean and the Adriatic Sea and about half way between Venice and Naples. It is about a two-and-a-half-hour drive to Rome or Florence. With motorways and the Autostrada reasonably close, there are a significant number of amazing destinations in all directions from Perugia where you can do one, two, or three-day outings.

Perugia is a hilltop town surrounded by lots of valleys and other hilltops. It is quite scenic, actually. The city of Perugia is about 167,000 inhabitants, but it feels a lot larger as you drive around the city. More than 40,000 of Perugia's inhabitants are students. With students, faculty, residents, and tourists, the city center is vibrant: shops and restaurants abound, and there is no shortage of architectural, historical, and artistic venues to explore.

Perugia is not a destination city like Venice or Florence or Rome, or a destination area like La Cinque Terre or the Amalfi coast, but it is convenient and turned out to be a delightful place to have as a base of operations. If interested, there are multiple YouTube videos about Perugia. Also, Netflix has a documentary about the trials and tribulations of Amanda Knox who lived in Perugia and was convicted, acquitted, re-convicted, and re-acquitted of her roommate's murder. The documentary has some very nice shots of the city and surrounding area.

Villa Nuba sits a little east and north of the Perugia city center. To get to the city center, you can drive, walk, or take the bus. On Saturday when we met Elisabetta for our tour, we drove up Via Giuseppe, a quite steep street, to the Etruscan Arch, one of the several portals through which you pass to enter the old city.

The Etruscan Arch is on the north, northeast side of Perugia. Just outside the Etruscan Arch is the Perugia University for Foreigners, and not too far before the arch is a three-level parking garage: two underground levels and one above ground. Since our minivan was large in comparison to most vehicles in this area, we chose the above ground level every time we parked here.

On Sunday, we revisited the city center but this time we walked from Villa Nuba to Porta Pesa, more on the east side, and entered the city from there, a good 45-minute walk in each direction. After exploring parts of the city again, we headed to one of the best restaurants in the city center for lunch, Ristorante La Taverna, which is just west from the Piazza Repubblica. This was another restaurant recommended by Dave and Joan, and one validated by numerous positive on-line reviews.

Any time we entered a restaurant, I would always ask in my primitive Italian if the dog was permitted. The La Taverna host, Josie, responded in English, "Absolutely he is allowed, but I am just not sure about you." I immediately liked the place. His next question was about the dog's name. When I said "Jack Daniels," Josie acted like we were long lost cousins returning from an extended absence.

The restaurant has three distinct seating areas, each one a little deeper into the restaurant. When I asked if we could be seated in an area where Jack might not bother folks, Josie escorted us to the third seating area, which had racks and racks of wine all along the rear and side walls, and curved brick ceilings like an ancient wine cellar, which it well could have been at one time.

We were alone for the first 30 minutes, allowing the wait staff to fawn all over Jack, but then the tables, probably eight in all, in our area started filling up. Shortly after we were seated, the executive chef and owner, Claudio Brugalossi, came to visit us. Gray hair and mustache, handsome and stockier than most Italian men we encountered, his English was perfect.

It turned out that Claudio was an executive chef for Hyatt hotels in Tampa, Miami, and most recently Atlanta. We had eaten several times at Armani's at the top of the Tampa Westshore Hyatt and advised him of that. As it turned out, Claudio started Armani's for Hyatt. After an exceedingly enjoyable visit, Kathy thanked Claudio for stopping by. His response: "I didn't come by to see you. I heard about Jack Daniels, and I wanted to meet him." How sweet. Now, we really loved this place.

And the dining experience? I successfully ordered a couple of glasses, not bicycles, of wine. Kathy had the chicken liver pâté on crostini (crostini di fegatini e balsamico), which she was instructed to eat with her fingers, and the spinach tortelloni (tortelloni di mozzarella e pomodoro al pesto di spinaci). I had the artichoke and lima bean soup (zuppa di fave e carciofi) and the black truffle ravioli (ravioli di tartufo nero al parmigiano). The meal was fabulous, only to be equaled by the nap that followed.

— § —

On Thursday, we went to the Rome airport via Pergola Bella to check in Jack for his stay at the pensione. It was bittersweet; happy to be on our way to Greece, but worried about our boy. The drive to Rome's airport was reasonably smooth, thanks to Giselle.

Since we had a French minivan, I named our GPS — Giselle. Giselle knew every country road, back road, dirt road, and alley in Italy. She took us on some routes where I thought we were turning into someone's farmhouse driveway. If I had a Euro for every time I said, "Giselle, you can't be serious," after receiving a command to turn here, I could afford to pay for Jack's veterinary bills.

Our stay at the Rome airport Hilton was enjoyable, and the next day we boarded our Aegean Airlines flight to Athens and then on to Thessaloniki. When we boarded the plane, I thought we had stepped onto a Pan Am flight from the 1960s. The flight attendants, five on each flight, were all female and dressed to the nines in sleeveless, dark blue dresses. Each one had her hair pulled back in a bun with a military style cap perched on top of her head.

Of the 10 total attendants, eight had jet-black hair. The other two were blonde. All had porcelain skin and wore bright red lipstick. They were all generally the same height, weight, and body shape, and all of similar age. They all spoke beautiful English, as well as Italian and Greek. The flights were great and the attendants were incredibly professional, courteous, and attentive. It was a bit of a surreal experience.

Thessaloniki is a city that has never been on my radar, and one I did not know how to properly pronounce until we got there. (It's THESS-uh-luh-NEE-Ki.) It is a port town of two million people located in the northeast corner of Greece. Our Australian/Greek friends had never been there and wanted to give it a shot. We came along for the ride.

Thessaloniki, like most of Greece, is still recovering from Greece's bankruptcy adventures with the European Union. The past eight or so years have been very tough for most Greeks. A lot of shuttered and dilapidated buildings dot the city's landscape, but this city appears to be climbing out of the ashes, if the crowds at the endless sidewalk cafés are any indication.

We stayed at the Met Hotel which is ultra-modern and quite spacious, though a little off the beaten path, but the hotel's complimentary shuttle service got us where we wanted to go. Our Australian friends flew from Adelaide to Sidney to Dubai to Athens to Thessaloniki, so when we met them Friday evening, they were exhausted and in favor of eating at our hotel.

The Food Channel has a recurring segment called *The Best Thing I Ever Ate*, and I felt like I could have contributed my appetizer for its consideration. Based on Theo's recommendation, he and I got the chargrilled octopus. The tentacle was about 10 inches in length, tenderized and marinated, and then grilled to perfection. Around the outside of the plate were islands of puréed fava beans and herbs, separated by small mounds of caviar.

The consistency and flavor of the octopus were amazing and the fava beans and caviar added such an explosion of taste that I mentioned a number of times "this has to be one of the best things I have ever eaten." I followed my appetizer up with grilled kingfish, sautéed spinach, and puréed peas, beautifully presented. Kathy had the grilled veal tenderloin, and Theo's wife, Heather, had the deconstructed moussaka – all to rave reviews.

While we had not seen many historical sites in our first three weeks in Italy and Greece, we were eating exceedingly well. But then, that is one of the reasons we came here.

CHAPTER FIVE

THESSALONIKI

SUNDAY, MAY 20 TO WEDNESDAY, MAY 23

I have always appreciated the fact that foreign travel has allowed me the opportunity to expand my knowledge of the culture, customs, and culinary traditions of the countries visited. This trip was no exception.

For example, when I mentioned the fava bean purée that was so magnificent with the chargrilled octopus, I misunderstood. The menu said "fava purée," which I assumed was made with fava beans. In Greece, according to Theo, fava purée is made mainly with split peas. You can find it made with fava beans or also with chickpeas, but that is less common. Some Greek culinary information for you.

Since we are in Greece, knowing the other characters in this Greek play may be helpful in understanding the vignettes that follow. Theodoro (Theo) is from the Greek island of Samos. He left with his parents and two siblings for Australia when he was three. Fliers promising work in the steel mills of South Australia had attracted his father to that area.

Within three months, his father broke his back working in the steel mill, and the family was left to fend for themselves. Theo started selling newspapers at five years old, and moved on to other entrepreneurial ventures from there. By the time he was 20, he had accumulated an estate of three quarters of a million dollars. Not bad for the 1970s.

He spent a sizable portion of his accumulated wealth on booze and gambling in his early 20s. Somewhere during this downward spiral, he met Heather and made a swift about face. He now owns one of the largest concrete companies in South Australia, a real estate development business, and a home building business. He has done well.

On Saturday, Theo said, "Let's go get some Euros." I thought to myself, "I have enough Euros, so what makes him think that I need more Euros?" With his Australian accent, Theo was actually saying, "Let's go get some gyros." For Greeks speaking English, the "g" is silent. The thought of gyros for lunch sent me desperately scrambling to find any excuse not to go along.

When I worked in London for more than a year, I passed lots of small street cafés, those with no or very limited indoor seating, that had these rotating blobs of "stuff" in their windows, from which they would cut pieces and deposit them into pita bread. To me it looked like hamburger mixed with sawdust and glue and shaped into a blob and then heated somehow. People actually paid money to eat the uniquely unappetizing and obviously unnatural stuff. Thank you, but no thank you.

Theo tried to educate me that I might be confusing shawarma meat, which is Lebanese and contains multiple kinds of meat, with gyro meat, which is Greek, and is either pork or chicken. Wanting to appear more worldly and adventuresome than I actually am, I agreed to give it a try. After all, when in Greece...Plus, since Kathy and Heather were already eager for gyros, I was not willing to suffer the ribbing I would be subjected to for wimping out.

Before leaving the hotel, Theo was able to get a line on the best gyro place in Thessaloniki – a recommendation that was later validated by a friend of his who was one of the distinguished chefs for the 2004 Olympics in Athens. We shuttled into the town center and then walked along a cement promenade, which is situated right at the water's edge, for an hour or so to build up our appetite. According to the taxi driver who gave us the ride from the airport, this promenade is the longest in Europe, and who am I to argue with a Greek taxi driver?

Around the middle part of the promenade is the entrance to a large plaza with green spaces and lined with high-end hotels on both sides. Heading up the gentle hill from the plaza is a very wide pedestrian street lined with shops, bakeries, cafés, and restaurants. The majority of the seating for these establishments was outside, and since this was Saturday afternoon, most places were crowded. The street reminded me of Las Ramblas in Barcelona, but on a much less sophisticated scale.

After passing several gyro places, we arrived at the recommended shop and found a line of folks waiting to place their orders, which we all interpreted as a favorable sign since the other gyro places had no such lines. I told Theo that I would defer to his expertise and would have whatever he ordered. I ended up with a pita filled with pork, onions, tomatoes, ketchup, mustard, and French fries: yep, French fries.

Eating a gyro this large like a hamburger or a taco was out of the question. Forks all around, and Greek beer to wash it down. I summoned up all the gastronomical courage I could muster, and dug in. To my surprise, it was delicious. Now I was intrigued by what I was eating and wanted to learn more.

The shop, which has only an ordering counter, had three large rotating spits, two with pork and one with chicken, with a large half-moon vertical infrared grill behind each spit. The folks working the counter told me they build their spits in the shop above the restaurant each day by layering very thinly cut and then pressed fresh pork or chicken on the spit's metal mesh base. Herbs and spices are added as the spit is built.

This process allows them to shape the gyro spit into as wide or narrow a spit as they want. It is all meat and only meat — no glue and sawdust here. It takes between one to two hours to build each spit. The spits are then frozen until needed, and they go through four to five spits a day.

The searing heat from the infrared grills cooks the outside quarter inch or so of the meat, while the rest of the meat stays cold or frozen until it is exposed to the searing heat. A very strong and healthy young man with a very sharp knife, unlike the ones at our home base Villa Nuba, stands watch over the spits, and when that outside layer is uniformly grilled, he artistically shaves off that quarter inch of grilled meat as the spit rotates.

The shaved meat then gets married in a pita with whatever additional ingredients the order calls for. This shop has several full-time runners who "scooter" gyro meals all over Thessaloniki.

Clearly, I have done Greeks and gyros a disservice by my former warped view of the food, and I have embarrassed myself by detailing my substantial lack of knowledge in such a public forum. My apologies to Greeks everywhere. To make up for my transgressions, I would be sure to enjoy one more authentic Greek gyro before I left Thessaloniki.

After the gyros, we returned to our hotel to meet some of Theo's "relatives" and friends. Like Theo, Dmitri, one of Theo's adopted relatives, was born in Samos but left for the island of Rhodes when he was 11 to find work. He built up a successful material and drapery business only to have it crumble almost to nothing when the Greek economy took a major down turn eight years ago. The adverse effect of the markets was exacerbated when Dmitri's son made some unwise real estate investments at the same time. Toula, Dmitri's wife, was with him.

Dmitri is the brother of the man married to Theo's cousin, who still lives in Samos. Along with Dmitri and Toula was another couple from Thessaloniki, whom Dmitri introduced as George and Kathy. Seriously, George and Kathy! George was in the same business as Dmitri, but Thessaloniki was his market area. Early on in their careers their paths crossed during a textile business conference. They hit it off and became life-long friends.

That evening, the eight of us went to dinner in a trendy part of the city filled with outdoor restaurants. Greeks are like Italians in many ways. They all talk at the same time, no one appears to be listening to what the others are saying, but everyone miraculously seems to absorb all the threads of conversation. Theo was exhausted from interpreting for us.

I would go over the outstanding meal we enjoyed, but it was overshadowed by the lunch we experienced the following day and the adventure involved in getting to the lunch venue. George wanted to take us to his favorite waterside beach restaurant, which was about an hour car ride away. George could take four in his vehicle, which meant we needed transportation for the other four. Dmitri, whose English is quite good, decided that he would step up and hire a car for the day.

After a lot of hand gestures and yelling on both sides of the phone line, the car rental representative hung up on Dmitri. The problem? Dmitri apparently can rent a car for the day in Rhodes for 30 Euro; but the guy on the other end would not budge from 60 Euro. Rather than deal with Dmitri, he hung up. To hell with the rental guy. We took a taxi.

Dmitri is one of the sweetest persons you will ever meet, and I am sure that he had no clue how far away the restaurant was from our hotel or how much the taxi bill would be. When the rental car negotiations came to an abrupt end, Theo, who is extremely generous when he comes to Greece, footing the bill for every meal or drink his Greek relatives and friends enjoy, offered to pay for the taxi. The trip cost over 45 Euro each way.

Instead of paying 60 Euro for a rental car, Dmitri let Theo pay 90 Euro for a taxi. This taxi vignette is a reflection of the state of affairs in Greece. It supports a common story I heard over and over from small entrepreneurs, including George, during our stay: too many folks trying to enjoy all the benefits they can at someone else's expense, with, according to some small business owners, government employees leading the way.

Some entrepreneurs see the philosophy of government employees as: if I don't have to pay for it, then it is not my problem. These same entrepreneurs think the Greek government has become so bloated and inefficient that its demand for funds is siphoning away precious capital needed by job creators. But surely, I digress.

Thessaloniki sits at the top center of a very large bay. Our restaurant destination was near the far end of the east side of the open horseshoe that forms the bay. From the waterside restaurant, you could look across the bay and see the neighborhoods of Thessaloniki rise up from the water's edge to the hills above.

Our restaurant, called the Gondola, was located in a seaside area called Perea. On the right side of the access road through Perea are the sand and the water. On the left side are homes and restaurants. While the restaurants have some limited indoor seating, most restaurants have very large white tents built on the sand with tables and chairs dispersed underneath. It really is a stunning setting, and the weather this time of year was magnificent for an outdoor lunch.

According to Theo, when Greek men eat seafood at lunch, Ouzo over ice is the preferred drink. Kathy and I opted for Greek beer since most "vino rosso della casa" we tasted in Greece had a sweet taste. When the owner/waiter, who has known George for a lifetime, asked what we wanted to eat, everyone took a shot or two at ordering their favorite dishes, with Dmitri's wife Toula leading the charge.

The square platters, and I mean platters larger than a standard large dinner plate, started to arrive in sporadic fashion. Two platters of toasted garlic bread, a platter of grilled octopus, a platter of fried shark steaks with garlic mash, a platter of roasted sardines, a platter of fried red baby mullet, a platter of fried calamari, a platter of Greek salad loaded with bricks of amazing feta cheese, a platter of eggplant salad, a platter of "sautéed grass with garlic" that was similar to spinach or collard greens or maybe kale.

It was true family style dining, and, as the meal progressed with platters being shared left and right, it looked like landings and takeoffs at Kennedy airport. Four small bottles of Ouzo, four beers, and countless bottles of water and the bill for eight people for this three-hour feast, which Theo and I split to thank our Greek friends, came to 130 Euro. It was as enchanting a setting and meal in a foreign country with locals as we have ever encountered.

CHAPTER SIX

CASTIGLIONE DEL LAGO — MONTEPULCIANO — MONTALCINO

WEDNESDAY, MAY 23 TO FRIDAY, MAY 25

O ur flights with Aegean Airlines from Thessaloniki to Athens and then to Rome were superb. We picked up our car from the Rome Airport Hilton Hotel parking lot and headed to pick up our boy Jack at Pergola Bella. The trip was about two hours and 15 minutes and involved no drama.

So, how was Jack when we picked him up after returning from Greece?

It had been raining in the local area, and Jack had been out enjoying the mud. I accompanied Loris back to Jack's large outdoor pen (a big mistake), and Jack was so happy to see me that he left a ton of muddy paw prints all over my jeans, shirt, and shoes. At reunions like this, it appears that all training goes out the window.

While we were happy to see our boy, we were less than pleased with the condition Jack's skin was in when we retrieved him from Pergola Bella. We were dismayed to find that his skin rash had returned with a vengeance. Apparently, Loris failed to notice the change in Jack's condition. More visits to Dr. Massimo were in our future.

Over Wednesday and Thursday, we communicated with Giuseppe to act as our intermediary to get an appointment with Dr. Massimo on Saturday. This timing was good because we would be checking back in to our home base at Villa Nuba Saturday afternoon.

Since we could not return to our Villa Nuba apartment until Saturday, I booked three nights at Hotel Aganoor in the town of Castiglione del Lago, which was only about 40 minutes away from Pergola Bella. Castiglione del Lago is a charming hilltop town that sits about in the middle of the west side of Lake Trasimeno. It is Giuseppe's favorite town on the lake. The fact that it is close to Montepulciano and Montalcino, two amazing hilltop towns with expansive and renowned wine growing areas, made it an easy pick as a place to spend three days.

The walled part of Castiglione del Lago is not all that wide, maybe three to four blocks or so, and only seven or eight blocks long. The small size makes it an ideal place to walk around and interact with the vendors, who all appear genuinely friendly. With any walled Italian city, the streets are narrow, and become more restrictive when dining tables and chairs are placed outdoors, barely allowing one vehicle to transit the street at a time. The entry doors for all the shops, restaurants and hotels are right on the street, so caution is warranted each time you pop out of a door. Hotel Aganoor has three doors: a door to the restaurant, one to the hotel office, and a separate large stable-like door to the stairs leading to the guest rooms.

At the end of the walled city near our hotel sat a hospital, large museum, and metropolitan offices all with a fair amount of green space for Jack to enjoy. Hotel Aganoor sits just a block up the narrow main street from the green space. There are set times when vehicles are allowed to be on the streets, so we were able to drive to the hotel entrance to unload our bags but had to exit to off street parking once that task was complete. In the evening, all the streets become pedestrian friendly.

Travelling abroad teaches tough lessons every now and then, and I have endured my fair share. Somehow, with the passage of time, those painful experiences fade in order to allow me to be punished all over again, as was the case here. The way my wife packs, it is always a wise move to get ground floor accommodations or else make sure the hotel has an elevator, a minor detail I overlooked. All the guest rooms at Hotel Aganoor are on the third floor (second floor to Italians), 44 steps each way. Needless to say, our three-day stay was an unanticipated and unappreciated opportunity to pad my step count.

Wednesday evening, we elected to dine at the hotel's Ristorante La Cantina. The restaurant has a quite charming indoor seating area with tall wine cellar-like curved brick ceilings. The outdoor seating area, perhaps larger than the inside, overlooks the northern half of Lake Trasimeno, which sits 100 feet or more below. We had insalata mista, a bottle of local red wine (gamay and cabernet grapes) recommended by our server, and then we split a pizza capriccioso. No disrespect to Il Cantinone in Perugia, but this was the best pizza we had eaten to date.

— § —

Thursday, we headed to Montepulciano, a mere 45-minute drive away. I love the way the town's name just rolls off the tongue. The town has intrigued me for decades because during that time, I have been enjoying various brands of Vino Nobile di Montepulciano.

Beautiful hilltop towns in Italy are like Baptist churches in South Carolina: they appear to be everywhere you turn. On the drive from Castiglione del Lago to Montepulciano, each time we came across a new vista there was, off in the distance, a hilltop town that we assumed was Montepulciano. Each time we were wrong – so many hilltop towns and so little time.

Unlike our good friends Ed and Liz, neighbors of ours in the Cliffs at Keowee Springs, who several years ago drove their rental car to the center of Montepulciano, ignoring at least a dozen signs warning "traffic strictly limited to residents with parking permits," and had a stressful time extricating themselves from the town's center, I found a parking lot not too far away. Besides, I wanted to avoid saying "Giselle, you want me to drive this wide minivan through that narrow 2,000-year-old arch? You can't be serious."

Not exactly sure where we were relative to the city center, we hiked our way up to a small piazza where I overheard two young American women chatting. I interrupted and asked for directions to the city center, which one of the young ladies provided. We had not progressed more than 50 yards when she caught up with us and explained that she was heading to her apartment and would be happy to escort us to the center since it was on the way. Jack was ecstatic to have some company.

It turns out that our new friend was from Georgia and was in Montepulciano on a study abroad program for a few months. For six blocks, we had our own private guide, during which time she recommended her favorite dress/clothing stores and restaurants. After wandering the town for an hour or so, Kathy got down to some serious clothes shopping, and then we went to lunch at Café Poliziano, Via Voltaia nel Corso 27, our student guide's favorite eatery.

Heading down a flight of stairs from street level to a strange restaurant that appeared to be below ground was not necessarily all that appealing, but we decided to go with the recommendation. As it turned out, the main downstairs restaurant was well lit because its entire backside was exposed, as in an opening in the side of a high cliff. We dined, somewhat nervously, on the overhanging veranda that provided wonderful views of the hills to the east of Montepulciano.

We started with bruschetta and a bottle of 2014 Valdipiatta Vino Nobile di Montepulciano, which was excellent. Kathy had the "pici cacio e pepe" – an alfredo-like dish made with "pasta of the house," pepper, pecorino-romano cheese, and a pound or three of butter. She enjoyed it so much, I thought she was re-enacting Meg Ryan's lunch scene at Katz's delicatessen in *When Harry Met Sally*. I had the pasta with wild boar sauce, which was very good, just not as climactic. We wandered a little more after lunch, then started the trek back to find our car, which we accomplished, and drove back to Hotel Aganoor.

Having a dog is a new phenomenon for me. When we lived in Ireland, my family had an Irish Setter but the dog passed away around the time I was five or six years old, so my memories are few and probably based on photos rather than personal experience. Jack has enriched our life and proven to be a delight, except when he isn't. All dog owners probably know what I mean.

I take Jack out to go potty before I head to bed, but usually once a night between 3:00 a.m. and 5:00 a.m., he comes into the bedroom, jumps on our bed and then paws me or licks my face to let me know that Mother Nature calls. It is really quite cute the way he does this, but I need to figure out how to get him to hold his business till a more reasonable hour.

With the return of Jack's rash came what I will describe as less than ideal consistency for the output of his digestive process. So, I started treating his need to visit the green area with a certain level of urgency. The night we returned from Montepulciano, we hit the hay a little early. Maybe it was jet lag that caused the early bedtime. Maybe it was being in the sun all day. Maybe it was the bottle of wine at lunch and the bottle of wine at dinner and the limoncello afterwards. But then, who really knows?

Anyway, true to his modus operandi Jack jumped on the bed and licked my face, tough to do since I wear a respiratory mask, to let me know it was that time of night. I donned my flip-flops and baseball cap and headed down 44 steps to the street. As I exited the large and very loud creaking hotel door, all eyes turned on me. It was shortly after 10:00 p.m. and the street was still filled with folks dining at sidewalk tables on both sides of the street.

I was wearing very loud yellow pajama pants emblazoned with multicolored shamrocks and black Guinness logos. Repeated washings had shortened the pajama legs to just above my ankles. To complete my ensemble, I had a seriously mismatched plaid pajama top, equally as garish. What to do? I could not abandon Jack in his time of need, so I pretended that I owned the street and the two of us pranced off to the closest green space to the staring eyes of a hundred evening diners. Poor Jack thought they were looking at him. The return journey was equally daunting. As we reentered the hotel, we may have received a round of applause, but I can't be sure because I was not wearing my hearing aids.

— § —

As I have matured, I like to think that my wine tastes have also matured. While my go to "spirit" has always been Jack Daniel's, my wine tastes have gone from merlot to cabernet to pinot noir. But over the last 10 years or so I have also developed an affinity for Italian wines, particularly Brunello de Montalcino. Brunellos are complex wines that need to be decanted and allowed to breathe for some time for their true character to emerge.

Back home in America, we live in the Cliffs at Keowee Springs, one of seven Cliffs golf communities in South and North Carolina. The Cliffs has a chief wine sommelier, Eric Cooperman, who buys wine in bulk from all over the world and then makes his purchases available to members on a first come first served basis.

One of his recent mailings was about a 2012 Brunello di Montalcino from Le Chiuse Vineyard. Never having heard of the vineyard, I purchased only three bottles. The wine evaluator's notes, which rated the wine at 96 points, said to hold until 2022 and then drink between then and 2037. Fat chance of that happening.

Shortly after my purchase, we attended a wonderful dinner party hosted by our good friends and fellow Keowee Springs residents, Michael and Ruth. With appetizers, Michael served some fine red wines but for the actual dinner he opened the Le Chiuse Brunello. Apparently, he was as impatient as I am. The wine was stunning, which compelled me to chart the vineyard's location for our upcoming trip.

The Le Chiuse Winery is about six miles from the town of Montalcino, and Montalcino is about an hour and 15-minute drive from Castiglione del Lago. The winery's website did not talk about wine tours or tastings, but I decided to head there on Friday regardless. Kathy and Jack decided to hang back.

The landscape I encountered on my drive was magnificent: rolling hills with elevation changes at every turn, wide vistas, farm lands full of grain, olive tree groves and grape vineyards dotting the hillsides, and long driveways lined with tall Italian cypress trees.

Giselle could get me to Montalcino but not to Le Chiuse, so I had to resort to my cell phone's Google map app, which got me close. After being deposited by Google on a gravel road, I was on my own to try and follow the suggested dotted line. A few gravel roads later and with help from locals, I made it to Le Chiuse, parked, and stuck my head in the first open door I could find, where I encountered a couple of vineyard workers who disappeared and returned with Lorenzo.

Lorenzo Magnelli, short, stocky, mid-30s with excellent English, apparently is the public face of Le Chiuse. I introduced myself and explained that I had great admiration for his wine. I mentioned my Cliffs connection, which elicited no response, and asked about tours and tastings. Lorenzo stated that all tastings are by appointment and that he had a reporter and wine tasters from *Wine Advocate* on their way for lunch and a tasting. I did my best to wrangle a seat at the tasting table, but he was not buying it.

He must have felt sorry for me – the tears streaming down my cheeks might have given it away – because he looked at his watch and said to follow him. We entered the tasting area that had three sections with a few doors exiting to places unknown. The section to the left had a small table, some occasional chairs, and a long ledge or shelf displaying various bottles of the vineyard's historical Brunellos.

The last section contained an enormous wine vat and what appeared to be antique wine making equipment. The center section had a long dining table with four lunch place settings at one end and several opened bottles of wine. One of the walls of this section was filled with plaques and certificates attesting to the excellent wine Le Chiuse produces. Lorenzo retrieved a couple of wine glasses from a cupboard and proceeded to educate me on his winery. We then started tasting from the previously opened bottles of wine situated on the lunch table.

First, a Vino Rosso di Montalcino made from clusters of large grapes that grow on the same vines as the grapes that make up the Brunello (really good). Next, we tasted the 2013 Brunello, to which several wine reviewers have awarded 100 points, made from the clusters of smaller grapes (wonderful). And, finally, a 2010 Brunello Reserve that would be released in 2020 (amazing).

With 2012 completely sold out, Lorenzo was willing to sell me three bottles of the 2013 Brunello and one bottle of the 2009 Brunello reserve. I mentioned that I might not live to 2022, let alone wait till then to consume the wine. His advice was to decant the wine for at least three hours before consuming. Lorenzo handed me his card and told me to call sometime to set up a more formal tasting.

With my mission accomplished, I headed up to Montalcino to re-explore the city center. We visited the town in 2016 with a guide, and I decided to try and retrace a few of our previous steps. While Montalcino may not be the most beautiful hilltop walled town in Italy, it is one of my favorites because the town is reasonably small, because of the 360-degree views the town affords, and because the way the land below the town unfolds before your eyes. I dined at La Taverna Del Panfilo, which was superb, and then headed back, with Giselle's help this time, to Castiglione del Lago.

CHAPTER SEVEN

A RASH DECISION & OUR FIRST BUREAUCRATIC ENCOUNTER

FRIDAY, MAY 25 TO SUNDAY, JUNE 3

We explored Castiglione del Lago a little more and, based on a recommendation from one of the shop owners, ended up dining at L'Acquario. The food and wine were excellent enough so that we would go there again.

The shopkeeper who recommended L'Acquario owns and operates her own ceramic store, which is across and down the street from Hotel Aganoor. Her store is called Stefania Ceramiche (www.stefaniaceramiche.com). While she owns and operates the store, she also designs, makes, paints, glazes, and then ships her creations all over the world. Choose the item(s) you like, and she will customize them to any other color scheme you see in her store.

When we first stopped in to Stefania's shop to look around during our initial walk through the town, she was less than enthusiastic. I assume this was because we were lookers and not buyers. When we returned on Saturday morning and started to purchase items, she started to warm up. By the time we left her store, she and Kathy were hugging and kissing on the cheeks and exchanging email addresses.

— § —

The drive back to home base Perugia was smooth, and we met Dr. Massimo and his delightful wife, Simona, at the appointed time. All the blood tests and other tests that he had previously run, led the good doctor to believe that Jack had an allergy to his food or to some of the treats we had been giving him.

Dr. Massimo ran an ultrasound on Jack's stomach and said there was a little inflammation but nothing too serious. A cortisone shot, an antibiotic shot, a prescription for more antibiotics, a prescription for Hills prescription dog food, and a nice large bill, and we were on our way back to our Villa Nuba apartment. Looked like I would be trading 75 Euro a bag dog food for 85 Euro a bag dog food. The image of that new Mercedes in my driveway was fading fast.

Those first three weeks at Villa Nuba had been a little difficult because we knew we had to be completely out of the apartment for the new guests to spend their week. We packed what we needed for Greece, and Giuseppe was kind enough to store the rest of our belongings. Now that we were back at Villa Nuba for five straight months, it was a lot easier to unpack and start to put all our belongings in locations other than our suitcases. With everything in its place, maybe not its final place, a sense of calm came over Lorena, and Jack seemed quite content to be back on his blanket-covered sofa bed.

Packing for a two-week or three-week or even a month long overseas trip has its challenges. But spending six months overseas introduces a whole new level of complexity. Clothes are not the issue. It is impossible to haul six months of shampoo, deodorant, soap, and other cosmetics to Europe, despite Lufthansa's generous weight allowance. We had to trust that we could find suitable replacement items in Italy.

The closest mall to us was Centro Commerciale Collestrada, which became our go-to place for many things. It has a large grocery store called COOP, much like a budget Whole Foods Market. The store has an amazing fresh fish and meat market, cheese market, veggie market, wine market, and met our basic food, drink, and cosmetic requirements.

While our health, beauty, and sustenance needs were under control, I eventually got to the point that I needed a haircut. I was beginning to look like a disheveled Willie Nelson. Back in the States, I had the same stylist/barber for the last four years, and now I had to trust my looks to a perfect stranger whose language I didn't speak. This was stress.

Before our trip to Greece, Kathy decided she needed a trim. Her hair was short anyway, and I could not see the need, but who am I to argue? She went online to Google Translate and carefully scripted what she wanted done so she could present her requirements to the stylist, and off we went to Centro Commerciale.

The one place where Jack was not allowed was a grocery store, so every time Kathy shopped for groceries, Jack and I lounged at the food court, at the same table, right on the aisle across from the patisserie. I had my cappuccino and cornetto, and Jack held court for all his new fans. This trip was no different.

Jack and I retired to our reserved table, and Kathy headed to the salon. I have never known her to take longer than 20 minutes for a cut, but it was more than an hour before she returned to the food court. She departed as Kathy Houlihan and returned as Lorena "Buzz Cut" Bobbitt-Houlihan. I thought that she had been inducted into the Italian Army. Jack even growled.

I was about to ask, in a very sensitive way of course, "What the hell happened to you?" But the play by play started before she sat down. The best I could offer was a weak, "I am sure it will grow back, honey." It was a rough few days. The good news was she probably wouldn't need another haircut before we left Italy.

— § —

According to Giuseppe, the government's reach into the lives of its citizens is extensive. If you rent an apartment to anyone for more than 30 days, you must draw up a special contract, and that contract must be registered with the government. Not only that, the person renting the apartment must go to the financial ministry and apply for a fiscal number.

As a six-month renter, I had to comply with the law. One morning, Giuseppe and I headed off to Umbria's fiscal ministry to register the contract and get my fiscal code. While the ministry office was in the middle of Perugia, upon entering it felt as if we had walked into a license branch at any stateside local Department of Motor Vehicles.

The office had an information desk where you explain your needs and get a number (Giuseppe needed two numbers). A large waiting area contained a massive screen with numbers inching up the screen. Once your number flashed, then the screen indicated which door to enter and which desk to visit.

We entered through door #2 and headed to desk #4 to get my fiscal code. The gentleman clerk checked my passport and made a copy of the page where the latest EU entry visa stamp appeared. He checked Kathy's passport. I then had to sign in a few places on the application that Giuseppe had previously prepared. Since U.S. citizens cannot stay in the EU for more than 90 days, I provided the clerk my EU/Irish passport.

Shortly thereafter, the clerk and Giuseppe, who had been chatting continuously throughout the visit, started to giggle profusely. Giuseppe turned to me and said that the clerk said something to the effect of, "After 90 days with his EU passport, he can leave, but his wife will be detained, which might work out to his advantage." How did he know about Lorena? I giggled profusely, and then the clerk and I fist bumped. International male bonding at its finest. It was a beautiful moment.

So now I have a unique Italian government fiscal code that is mine for the rest of my life. "What is it good for?" I asked Giuseppe. Apparently, if I ever rent another place in Italy for more than 30 days, I won't need to go through this process again. Or if I start a business in Italy or if I decide to pay taxes to the Italian government, I can do so with my new fiscal code. The chance of that happening is about the same as my waiting until 2022 to drink my Le Chiuse Brunello.

After being back in the waiting area for 10 more minutes, we entered through door #1 and headed to desk #29, where we completed the rental contract registration process. With all the paperwork completed, about a two-hour ordeal, we left to go to another of Giuseppe's favorite patisseries for cappuccino and cornetto, and to contemplate the merits of the proposal from the gentleman behind desk #4.

— § —

During our last visit to Dr. Massimo, we scheduled an appointment for Jack for the following week to see what effect the shots, the antibiotics, and food swap might be having on Jack's rash. On the follow-up visit, it was clear the condition had not gotten worse. While still visible all over his back and neck, the rash seemed to be lessening but not fast enough for us. The consistency of Jack's stools had been slowly improving.

As a precaution, the doctor tested Jack for Canine Leishmania, a disease caused by sand flies biting infected dogs or other animals and transmitting the disease to dogs they bite later on. This disease is not common in the United States but is prevalent in the southern Mediterranean. Monday, we would get the results. If infected, there is no cure, just medicines to control the condition. If not infected, then Jack could be vaccinated against the condition, which, according to my research, is about 85 percent effective.

According to Alexander Graham Bell, when one door closes, another door opens. You just need to look. And as we were looking at the bulletin board in Dr. Massimo's office for information on a pet pensione closer to Villa Nuba, we noticed a flier for a dog sitting service from a person named Sofia. Turned out that Sofia was a college student and lived in the same building as Dr. Massimo's office.

One morning, we met Sofia for a meet and greet. Her English was quite good, and she and Jack seemed to get along. Early that afternoon, we scheduled a trial run for a few hours. When Kathy and I returned from lunch at Il Cantinone, neither Jack nor Sofia seemed worse for the wear.

Based on these results, we scheduled an evening appointment a few days later, so we could go back to dinner at La Taverna. Claudio and his staff remembered us, or perhaps the fact we were the two folks with Jack. They welcomed us but were openly disappointed Jack was not with us.

— § —

Some updates on items covered in the previous pages. First, we tried desperately and found that there is nothing you can do to improve the taste of unsalted Umbrian bread. Toasted with butter and jam won't do it. Olive oil and balsamic vinegar won't do it. Making garlic bread with it won't improve its taste.

Second, the Limonce limoncello I waxed so eloquently about and Italy's #1 seller had become suspect. After our experience at Ristorante Da Elio, I bought a bottle of Limonce and placed it in the freezer. The next night when I went for my post meal digestif, the limoncello was semi-frozen, like a snow cone, and would not dispense into a glass. Someone at the factory had been cutting back on the grain alcohol. Thereafter, two different limoncello brands occupied our freezer.

Third, in the "for what it's worth-less" category, Italian men of all ages do not wear golf or baseball hats. Every time I visited the mall or walked around any city, if I was wearing a hat, then I was the only one wearing a hat. Wearing a hat probably shouted, "I am an American." I hope it did not shout, "I am an ugly American."

Finally, what about the oven that was supposed to be in our apartment when we returned from Greece? I was not about to let Giuseppe pick out an oven for chef Kathy, and have the event trigger World War III. Before heading to Greece, I negotiated with Giuseppe that Kathy and I would pick out and purchase the oven, and he could reimburse us later.

CHAPTER EIGHT

SPELLO – PARCO CINOFILO – ASSISI

MONDAY, JUNE 4 TO SUNDAY, JUNE 10

D r. Massimo's office sits on a side street just off Via Eugubina, the road we took to get up to the city center. The office, which sits back about 10 yards from the street and is part of a tall apartment building, is plain looking. A single glass door on the left provides access to a small waiting area, maybe six feet deep and 10 feet wide. The waiting area is to the right of the entry door. The door to Massimo's interior office is directly opposite the entry door.

When we arrived for our follow up appointment, the waiting area was crowded: a couple with two teacup sized dogs, two guys with a cat in a crate, and a couple with a rather large dark-haired collie type dog that just wanted to bark at Jack. Due to the heat, the outside door was propped open. The couple with the large dog exited the waiting area, and Jack and I took their place at the far-right end.

Some minutes later, Dr. Massimo appeared through his interior door and called for Jack. We stood up and moved toward the good doctor at which point Jack made a bee line for the outside door, tail between his legs. Everyone in the waiting area appreciated the move, including the doctor.

And who can blame Jack? In the month we had been there, Jack had been given four shots, had a large thermometer inserted in his private area an equal number of times, had blood taken twice, and had to be restrained for an ultrasound of his stomach. On his first visit, Jack was muzzled because the doctor did not know what a sweet dog Jack was. Now, whenever I would lift him up on the examination table, he would start to tremble. It broke my heart.

But this trip produced good news. The test from Saturday showed that Jack had not been infected with Canine Leishmania. As a result, he was vaccinated against the disease, needle number five, for a mere 70 Euro. The Mercedes that was disappearing from my driveway appeared to be materializing in Dr. Massimo's driveway.

— § —

If you survey folks who have visited Italy at length or visited Italy frequently but for shorter periods, and ask them to list their favorite Italian towns, the town of Spello may not show on their list. Spello is about 30 minutes from Perugia, in the same direction as Assisi. In fact, you see Assisi up on the hillside to your left as you head to Spello.

Like many Italian towns, each year Spello hosts its own unique festival. The Spello festival is called Infiorata – Festival of Flowers, which celebrates the feast of Corpus Domini – the Body of Christ. Think Tournament of Roses floats without the moving floats. Groups plan their designs months in advance and procure the flowers needed to bring their designs into reality. Flowers, flower petals, tweezers, and glue are the paint, and the street is the canvas.

The streets are cleared the night before, and then large tarps are draped over each group's secret piece of real estate. Underneath the tarps people work through the night to craft their floral masterpiece. The tarps are removed around 7:00 a.m., and then crowds from all over Italy descend on Spello to admire.

We decided to head to Spello a few days before the Infiorata to check out the town. Spello has a very nice feel about it. It appears very clean. One of the reasons it seems clean is that most of the walls and buildings seem to be cut from the same stone type and color, and the buildings don't appear to be built over decades with each block having a different architecture than the previous block. It has a high level of consistency in its architecture, more so than we have experienced in other hilltop walled towns.

The other aspect of Spello we liked was the town was not crowded at all. We were able to wander at our leisure and pop in and out of shops without dodging other tourists, which led me to think that we might be able to get a room for Saturday evening, and then be up early on Sunday morning to watch the unveiling. Foolish me. All the hotels, and we hit three of them, were booked one to two years in advance of the festival.

One of the hotels we visited was Hotel Ristorante La Bastiglia. The hotel sits on the upper, as in uphill, end of Spello, in one of the highest areas of the city. It also sits on the edge of a precipice. It has a magnificent outdoor dining patio that overlooks the valley floor below and the mountains off to the east. While we did not dine there, the restaurant has received high praise. We shall return there.

We thought about returning Sunday morning to see the works of art, but then I started to envision a *Seinfeld* episode, where Jack got loose and gleefully romped his way through acres of flower designs, resulting in our being chased down the hillside to our car by a hysterical group of floral artisans carrying sharp tweezers and hot glue guns.

Truth be told, I spent most of Sunday in bed with clogged sinuses, a headache, and a cough and sore throat. It truly was a missed lifetime opportunity. If you go to YouTube and search for Infiorata di Spello, you will get some amazing videos of the floral arrangements from previous years.

— § —

Before our trip to Spello, Giuseppe and I went to another pensione, Parco Cinofilo Umbro, located in the countryside west and south of Perugia, not quite as far away as Pergola Bella. A brother and sister team, Matteo Ferracci, a dog trainer, and his sister Flavia, the administrator, operate Parco Cinofilo. Fortunately for me, Flavia spent three years in Australia, and she speaks beautiful English, so communicating about Jack was a breeze.

The facility was a little smaller than the previous pensione but appeared better suited for Jack's needs. The training facility had all the obstacles you see dogs navigating during the Westminster Kennel Dog Show. We booked Jack for four separate stays: the week we would be in Munich to attend a birthday celebration, the week Dave and Joan were planning to visit us for the Umbria Jazz Fest, the week we planned to visit Dublin, and the week we would be in Venice. Fingers and toes were crossed that this pensione would work out for our needs and Jack's well-being.

— § —

If you are Catholic like me, then St. Francis of Assisi (1181 to 1226) is a revered religious icon you were exposed to early in your Catholic education. He lived an amazing life in service to the church and service to its people (after an early life as a well-to-do spoiled young man). He founded the Franciscan Order, was beatified, then canonized as a saint, and became the patron saint of animals and patron saint of Italy. But his life is often characterized as so much more.

There is a quote, not grounded in historical fact, attributed to St. Francis that says: "Preach the gospel at all times. When necessary, use words." Those who have documented his life write that while the quote can't be proven as that of St. Francis, it was the kind of thing he would say. Soft and warm, gracious and caring, sensitive and wise, fearless and focused, intellectual and holy, he became the kind of person within whose expansive shadow one could easily dwell.

I found it interesting that, as a young man, Francis joined a local army to fight against the city of Perugia. Sometime during one of the battles, he was captured and imprisoned in Collestrada, the place where our favorite shopping mall was located. Apparently, it was this period of imprisonment that started Francis reflecting on the type of life to which he later dedicated himself.

It was with such educational memories and sense of awe that we headed to Assisi. The city is about four to five times as long as it is wide and easily walkable from end to end. We parked on the far south end at Piazza Matteotti, which is uphill from the town center. So, the trip into the city center was great, but the return trip, not so much.

Giselle took us well past the city and brought us to the last of three highway exits for Assisi. She took us east into the hillside and then back north through rolling hills of olive groves. Somehow it felt like a beautiful, serene, and fitting way to approach the city of Assisi.

An infinite number of sources will tell you when a city was founded and by whom, who then destroyed the city and who rebuilt it, what buildings are there today, how old they are, and what art works reside therein. All of this is important for sure. For me, the *vibe* of the city is also important. What is your gut reaction when you enter a beautiful walled hilltop town in Italy? What's your sense of what makes this town tick? Why do people live there? Why do people visit there?

Le Cinque Terre has a vibe, as do Siena, Montepulciano, and Montalcino, and yet each vibe is a little different based on the geographical, architectural, or agricultural feature for which the area is most noted. Assisi felt a little like Spello: clean with similar architecture throughout, common look and color to the stone used in its buildings, organized, not haphazard for a city more than 2,000 years old. The fact that it was rebuilt in parts over the centuries may explain.

At the same time, as we walked into the city, I sensed, with no empirical, scientific, or research basis whatsoever, an overall calmness and feeling of reverence about and within the people here, residents and visitors. It was as if everyone in Assisi was there to honor, appreciate, and stand in awe of the persona of St. Francis of Assisi, or there out of great but genuine curiosity concerning all the hype about this legendary Patron Saint of Italy. I was emotionally touched by the visit without entering a single building.

Chapter Nine

Cortona — Bureaucracy, Round Two

Monday, June 11 to Thursday, June 14

The ride to Cortona was quite pleasant. We drove through Perugia to the west side of the city where we picked up and followed the RA6 motorway, which took over the north end of Lake Trasimeno, for about 20 kilometers. Once off the motorway, the route to Cortona was a two-lane road through gentle rolling hills. The road eventually turned into a series of steep switchbacks that led us up to the city's perimeter.

With more than a month of driving in Italy under my belt, I learned a few things. First and foremost, before you go anywhere, figure out where to park. We had reasonably good Internet service at Villa Nuba, so Googling the best places to park was invaluable. There are any number of sites that will offer the advantages and disadvantages of each of the designated parking areas. Since parking inside hilltop walled towns is generally reserved for residents, most visitor parking lots are below, sometimes well below, the city center.

The second thing I learned is to take a list of the top four to six best places to dine for lunch or dinner, depending on the timing of the visit. Like most folks, I build my list by selecting those restaurants that make the top 10 on at least two but preferably three dining review sites. While we did dine on the fly a number of times and were not overly disappointed, selecting from the list of highly recommended establishments truly enhanced our culinary experiences.

Giselle did her usual magnificent job of getting us to the parking area near Piazza Garibaldi, which has an elevated semicircular drive, with a stone railing overlooking the valley to the south and west of the city. Half a dozen artists with easels and paints lined the shaded sidewalk along the edge of the curved stone railing, each person capturing differing aspects of the valley below and mountains in the distance. It reminded me of walking along the Seine in Paris and seeing artists lining the bank, capturing their unique version of Notre Dame.

I also learned that my expectations, or perhaps lack of them, can color my actual experiences. I had no expectations, great or otherwise, regarding Spello and was most pleasantly surprised. Likewise, no real expectations were there for the town of Assisi, other than knowing in advance the town was all about the life of St.

Francis. Again, I was pleasantly surprised. On the other hand, I had high expectations for the city of Cortona, probably from having read back in the 2005 timeframe Frances Mayes' book *Under the Tuscan Sun*.

After spending three plus hours wandering the city, I was left wanting. The town was quite crowded with tourists, many probably with the same expectations as I, and there seemed to be an abundance of souvenir shops, even on Via Nazionale, which begins right at Piazza Garibaldi, and is one of the longest, most level, and most popular shopping streets in town. The east and north sides of Cortona are significantly more hilly than other walled towns we have visited, and don't seem to have an abundance of venues to attract tourists, hence the tourist overpopulation in the western third of the city.

In my view, Cortona is not as beautiful and its architecture is not as magnificent as other hilltop towns. The views from the city are not as majestic as those from Montalcino or Montepulciano. In comparison to other towns, its layout feels overly haphazard. Other than the western third of the town, it is physically difficult to navigate. Finally, it has been described by some as earthy and gritty – I can't say it was dirty, so I will just say it was not pristine. Am I glad we went? Yes. Would I return? Maybe, but not until after we had visited the other hilltop towns on our to-do list.

There is no love lost between Umbrians and Tuscans, as Giuseppe Nuzzaci loved to point out at any and every opportunity. Umbria is the breadbasket of Italy and believes that it should get equal billing with Tuscany. However, most Umbrians believe Tuscany gets all the glory just because of "wine."

Cortona at one point in its early history actually belonged to Umbria. After a few years, it ended up right across the border in Tuscany, so it is just barely "under the Tuscan sun." When I mentioned to Giuseppe that we spent the day in Cortona, he replied, "Cortona used to be in Umbria, but we got rid of it." Spoken like a true Umbrian.

On the brighter side, we had a wonderful dining experience in Cortona. Since we arrived mid-morning and did most of our exploring early, we sat at an outdoor wine bar in the Piazza Della Repubblica, gave our feet a break, had some Italian chardonnay, and watched a continuous parade of fellow tourists. By the time we were ready for lunch, our primary choice, La Bucaccia, was not open, so we opted for Osteria Del Teatro, just off Piazza Signorelli.

We found that the interiors of many fine-dining restaurants inside these walled towns were splendid, and the Osteria was no exception. Because the restaurant is so close to the Signorelli Theater, it is one of the preferred pre-theater and post-theater dining venues. The interior, with beautiful wall and ceiling beams, is adorned with photographs of theater stars and well-heeled theater patrons. We were seated at a rear corner table so Jack could keep his eye on our fellow diners. Thankfully, he was quite tired from traversing the city's steep terrain and slept peacefully on the cool tile floor.

We ordered some local area red wine and then got down to the serious business of scrutinizing the menu. An appetizer that neither one of us had ever heard of caught Kathy's eye – an asparagus flan. For me, the word "flan" conjured up thoughts of dessert, not appetizer. Realizing I needed to expand my culinary repertoire, I reluctantly acquiesced to splitting the appetizer.

The asparagus appetizer and arrived, and it turned out to be "one of the best things I ever ate." The flan itself was in the shape of a hockey puck, perhaps slightly larger. Attached around the edge of the flan were asparagus spears, and then on top were thin slices of grilled guinea hen. The flan's consistency was firm, not soft or mushy, so it was easy to cut and held together well, and the flan was hot, as if just removed from an oven. The flan sat on a generous bed of slightly warm, soft Italian robiola cheese that for me made the dish great. The explosion of flavor from the cheese, hot flan, and grilled meat was amazing. It was truly an "OMG this is so good" moment.

— § —

This Italian sojourn was not all fun. Our trips to idyllic destinations got interspersed with doses of reality (laundry, cleaning, cooking, and napping), and a sobering dose of Italian bureaucracy. Everyone else's bureaucracy is fair game for ridicule, and during my lifetime, I have done my fair share of ridiculing. On the other hand, based on the companies within which I have worked, organizations recoil at criticism of their own bureaucracy, which they believe to be necessary, minimalist, streamlined, effective and efficient. Italian bureaucracies bear no resemblance to the five preceding adjectives.

The hassle that I went through bringing Mister Jack to Italy pales in comparison to the hassle I began to experience to get Miss Kathy's residency card. United States citizens cannot stay longer than 90 days in the Schengen Area of the European Union, which includes all the countries we had or would be visiting on this six-month holiday. Since I have an EU/Irish passport, the issue does not affect me. I could go wherever I wanted and stay and long as I wanted, and no one would care. Kathy, who was not working and not there as a student, was a different story.

In anticipation of the challenges we were about to face, before leaving the U.S. I completed the visa request for family members, and months in advance booked an appointment at the Italian consulate in Coral Gables, Florida, which handles the southeast region of the United States. The trip to Florida involved two round trip airline tickets, two nights in a hotel, a rental car, meals, and boarding for Jack. The shopping Kathy did at a mall in Coral Gables was collateral damage.

We arrived 15 minutes ahead of our appointed time and checked in with the consulate clerk. A while later, we were escorted along with 40 of our closest friends to a compact room on the third floor of the consulate, where three clerks behind bulletproof glass took turns calling out names of folks to be serviced. The room was so cozy that every person in the room was privy to every conversation at every window.

Finally, our names were called. Having rehearsed my preamble as to why we were there, I was prepared with my story upon reaching window #3. The clerk stopped me after a couple of minutes into my monologue. Having simultaneously brandished my EU passport and my wife's U.S. passport at the start of my diatribe, the clerk easily diagnosed my problem. He handed me a typed paper that read: "Family members of EU citizens no longer need a visa to stay more than 90 days in Italy. They will enter as a tourist, without a visa, and then request the residency card (carta di soggiorno) while in Italy."

At that moment, I understood more fully the term mixed emotions. Realizing that I needlessly spent $2,000 on this trip, I wanted to reach through the bulletproof glass and choke the life out of clerk #3. On the other hand, I was happy that such a complex issue had been boiled down to a simple "request the residency card while in Italy." Kathy's residency hurdle had been overcome by two simple sentences printed on a piece of white paper. Our new challenge, once in Italy, would be to find the correct office in Perugia that issues residency cards. Simple enough.

— § —

Riding through the streets of Perugia as a passenger in Giuseppe Nuzzaci's car could be classified as a significant emotional event. Sometimes he was looking at the road, but mostly not. Sometimes his hands were on the wheel, but mostly not. All the time he was talking, looking at me, and touching my shoulder to emphasize a point, usually something about his ex-wife and their current divorce proceedings. Despite repeatedly thrusting my right foot though the floorboard of Giuseppe's car, 20 minutes later we arrived unscathed at the headquarters of the Perugia Branch of the Polizia Nazionale, the organization that issues residency cards.

In and out in a flash, we thought. I have my EU passport. I have my registered rental agreement. I have my permanent Italian fiscal code. Get the form we need to fill out and return it the next day along with my spouse, her passport, and some photos. Simple enough, or so we thought. We were politely informed that I (yes, me the guy with the EU passport and the lifetime Italian fiscal code) needed to prove that I was a resident of Italy before any "carta di soggiorno" would be issued. You can't be serious?

Great. So, who was the person who handles that? "We don't do that here. The administrative office of the City of Perugia does residency certifications." Off we headed on another 20-minute white-knuckle drive to the administrative office of the City of Perugia where we got married up with clerk #5. By now you have figured out that Giuseppe did all the talking and hand waving. I sat by, nodded, smiled occasionally, and tried to look desperate and pathetic when needed.

Clerk #5 was sweet and sympathetic and understanding, but not very helpful. She handed us two separate single page forms and an eight-page form to fill out. She scheduled an appointment for us for June 28, at which time we were to return the completed forms and supporting documentation. If all went well at that time, we would get "something" to take back to the Polizia Nazionale attesting to my residency. What about my recorded rental agreement and my lifetime fiscal code? Didn't that prove I was a resident? Ah, that. Well, not with them – that involved someone else's bureaucracy.

In the interest of efficiency, we went back to Polizia Nazionale to make sure we understood the next steps. This time we headed to the information office rather than the office filled with clerks carrying guns behind bulletproof glass. The lady operating this one-person office was truly helpful. She gave us a checklist of all the items we would need to bring with us for the residency card, partially completed a form that we needed to return in a couple of days, scheduled an appointment for us on July 24, the 89th day we would be in the Schengen area, and gave us the office we needed to go to have an official translation done of our marriage certificate.

— § —

Weeks ago, on my solitary drive from Castiglione del Lago to Montalcino and back, I had a momentary vision of what it would be like to drive those same beautiful winding roads in my Boxter GTS convertible. And I was temporarily lost in the happiness of that thought. But then I realized that I would have to give up two thirds of my luggage, give up my wife and all her luggage, and give up my dog and all his luggage. And it seemed that might be a bridge too far. After this exhausting day dealing with the Italian bureaucracy, and my previous experience with Jack and all his issues, the sacrifice suddenly did not seem all that onerous.

Chapter Ten

Bologna

Thursday, June 14 to Monday June 18

In all my years of European travel, maybe 15 trips or more to Europe, not counting working in London for more than a year and working in Frankfurt for three and a half years, I have opted, where possible, for visiting the smaller towns and cities. To me, navigating the smaller venues was easier, the experiences more memorable, the people friendlier, the scenery more dramatic, and the food and drink of equal – sometimes better – quality.

As a result, I built an unfounded, irrational, and quite unsophisticated bias against large cities for being too crowded, too noisy, too dirty, and too difficult to navigate by car to make the effort worthwhile. Even on all my trips to my homeland, I avoided Dublin like the plague for all the reasons just stated.

However, several years ago on a trip to Ireland, because of our itinerary, we needed to kill a few days, and Dublin, for logistical reasons, was the place where we needed to spend the time. After a day on the hop-on, hop-off bus, and another day exploring Dublin on our own, I fell in love with my old capital city, and my big city bias started to dissipate.

On this Italian holiday, I knew there would be the obligatory trip to Rome where we would hit all the tourist spots and then head out of town as soon as practical. Milan, Bologna, Florence, and Naples were not on my immediate radar screen. And then we went to Greece. And in the seat pocket in front of me was the Aegean Airlines flight magazine, one of whose lead stories was about Bologna, the gastronomical capital of Italy.

The more I read the 10-page article, the more I became intrigued with Bologna. Further, having now spent seven weeks with Giselle, I was feeling very confident that navigating to and within Bologna would not be an insurmountable task. So off we headed, armed with the Aegean Airlines magazine, for four days to explore Bologna's gastronomical hotspots.

When I plugged an address into Giselle, she did not hesitate to plot her desired route. No alternate routes were offered. They may have been available. I just didn't know how to find the feature or how to get it to work, if it did exist.

Regardless, other than not being able to find Le Chiuse vineyard, Gisele had been amazingly accurate, so I became accustomed to trusting her implicitly.

Giselle got us from our home base apartment in Perugia to our hotel in Bologna in just a little over three hours. We headed generally in the same direction as our trip to Cortona but followed the RA6 until it intersected with the A1 towards Florence. What Giselle failed to mention is that when all was said and done, we would end up paying over 30 Euro in tolls and transit 44 tunnels between Florence and Bologna alone.

Several of these tunnels are more than a mile long, and one tunnel was nearly five miles long. Poor Jack. With 44 periods of darkness interspersed with brief periods of light, he was not sure if he should be getting up or going to bed. Poor Dan. With the road between Florence and Bologna being the busiest truck route in Italy and with more than 90,000 vehicles a day making the trip, it was an intense driving experience. The adult beverage at the end of the road was well deserved, much appreciated, easily consumed, and quickly repeated.

Most of our hotel loyalty points are with Hilton Hotels. When Hilton had no properties at my desired location, I used Expedia, and it worked out well. For our four days in Bologna, we selected the Royal Hotel Carlton. The hotel was delightful, the staff very accommodating, and the property had ample green space to accommodate our boy Jack. It is funny how Jack has changed my hotel booking approach. Now before I book a hotel, I use the satellite view to see how far I am going to have to walk in pajamas to find green space. No attached or close green space? No reservation.

The Royal Hotel Carlton is about four blocks from the main train station, but towards the direction of the city center. During our stay, we walked to the city center on several occasions. One block from the hotel to Via Dei Mille, left two blocks to Via Dell'Indipendenza, right about 12 blocks to Via U. Bassi. In all, about a 15 to 20-minute walk one way.

Once at the intersection of Via U. Bassi and Via Indipendenza you are in the heart of the city center and in the midst of a plethora of amazing eateries, a number of which are located down these really narrow alleyways, and an array of beautiful historical buildings.

On our last day, we took the hop-on, hop-off bus around and through the city to get a better perspective of Bologna. I liked what I saw. What is really enjoyable about Bologna is that on Saturday and Sunday, both Via U. Bassi and Via

Indipendenza become pedestrian only thoroughfares, and the crowds that show up appreciate that fact.

Since we did not check into our hotel until Thursday afternoon, we had a late lunch at Trattoria Bolognese, a plain and unassuming restaurant but a delightful find on Via Dei Mille within a few blocks of our hotel. That evening we dined at our hotel restaurant, which turned out to be pricey but the food was of excellent quality. All things considered, Trattoria Bolognese was more enjoyable.

Those of you who follow Italian chefs and Italian cooking know of "Eataly." Joan, of "I thought that there was an oven in my Villa Nuba apartment" fame and Mimi, another friend, introduced Kathy to the Chicago Eataly during a Keowee Springs ladies trip to Chicago that Joan and Mimi organized. Apparently, at the Chicago Eataly it was love at first bite. There is an Eataly in Rome and one in Florence, which we have visited, but the granddaddy of them all is Eataly World in Bologna, and we headed there on Friday.

It is hard to do justice to Eataly World. It encompasses 100,000 square meters of covered space. There are 100 vendors inside the complex and 42 restaurants. The approach to Eataly World is like the approach to the Magic Kingdom at Walt Disney World.

Dedicated highways, huge directional signs, multiple parking lots, and motorized choo-choo trains to get you from your parking lot to the complex entrance guarantee you won't get lost. Once inside, you can check out a three-wheeled bicycle, with baskets fore and aft for your purchases, to help you traverse the enormous complex.

At the entrance of Eataly World is a massive store that appears to have products on display from all 100 on-site vendors, plus many other Italian companies. So, if you want to go no farther, you can probably purchase all things Italian right there. As you leave the store and venture farther into the bowels of the complex, you start to encounter the individual vendors.

There are displays about how things are grown, how meats are cured, how pasta is made, how grapes are processed, how olives are pressed, how cheese is aged. Vendors from north, south, east, and west are represented, each with a compelling story as to why their product is worth your attention. Interspersed between the vendor displays and shelves of products are eateries devoted to products respective to their immediate region.

Walking Eataly World is more mentally taxing than physically exhausting. Think about the first floor of any mall in the United States with 100 shops, without

59

walls, but all the shops are devoted to Italian food and wine. It is akin to traversing a library and fretting about how in the world you are supposed to read all those books. The Irish version of Eataly would fit in our kitchen at Villa Nuba. It would contain a pound of butter, a slab of bacon, a dozen eggs, a loaf of soda bread, a bag of potatoes, a cut of meat for stew, a case of Guinness, and a bottle of Jameson.

Every restaurant in Eataly World appears as equally attractive and compelling as the last. Out of desperation, not really, we stopped at an eatery sponsored by a Fattoria known for its cured meats and cheeses. The offer was a charcuterie board for two and a bottle of wine for 22 Euro. It was as delicious as it was economical.

We explored a little more and then succumbed to an offer of "tagliatelle cacio e pepe" several hundred yards farther down the complex. It too was delicious. After another hour of gazing, grazing, and grabbing, we returned to our hotel for a well-deserved nap.

The portico or covered sidewalk is a landmark of Bologna. These porticos are about three times the width of a standard sidewalk in the United States and reach a height of two stories. The majority of the buildings in central Bologna have porticos, and most buildings are only five or six stories tall.

Above the porticos are living or office or retail spaces. To the non-street side of the portico are shops, restaurants, and offices. The portico floor may be covered in granite, or marble, or terrazzo, or mosaic tile of some kind. The ceilings may or may not be adorned with frescoes. Some of the porticos on Via U. Bassi and neighboring streets contain the equivalent high-end shops you would find on Rodeo Drive.

Regardless, these porticos keep you out of inclement weather or blistering sunshine, and over 25 miles of porticos are dispersed throughout Bologna. Fortunately for us, we had absolutely perfect weather for our four days in Bologna, so the porticos never became a haven from the weather. The temperature was in the low 70s, there was not a cloud in the sky, the humidity was non-existent, and a gentle breeze was our constant companion.

Despite Rick Steves granting Bologna a mere single paragraph on page 207 of his 2015 Italy Guide, we enjoyed Bologna. You do have to overlook the overabundance of graffiti, the mildly littered streets, and the occasional panhandler. That said, we enjoyed our spaghetti "con frutti di mare" at Trattoria Bolognese, our pizza at Scalinatella, our mussels in spicy tomato sauce at Ristorante Pescatore, and our lunch at Baita La Vecchia Malga. I am glad we came here, and I would return. Kathy is still contemplating.

CHAPTER ELEVEN

TO MUNICH AND BACK

MONDAY, JUNE 18 TO WEDNESDAY, JUNE 27

O n Tuesday, our boy Jack was back at Dr. Massimo's office for another round of "let's hope we can find a cause and cure for Jack's rash." The rash had not gotten worse, but it had not gone away. When parts of his skin would clear up, it appeared that other body parts would break out with the rash. So far, we had eliminated an allergy to the shampoo used by Upstate Dog Training and an allergy to the type of food he was eating. Canine Leishmania, the Mediterranean sand fly disease, was eliminated via blood test.

On this visit, the good doctor did a second biopsy of one of the bumps on Jack's skin, and it proved negative once again for any kind of insect infestation. Now Dr. Massimo thought that Jack's rash might be an allergic reaction to the fleas or ticks that exist in Europe, and that the NexGard, which Jack takes every month, may not be potent enough. So, the doctor applied a solution of Bayer Advocate to Jack's neck and upper back. We would return in a week to assess progress and grasp at more straws.

— § —

The Citroen car lease program is good for a maximum of 165 days for any single lease. Because we were in Europe for more than 190 days, we had to have two separate leases for two separate brand-new cars; one lease in my name and one lease in Kathy's. Kathy would not drive in Italy, and either kept her eyes closed or held her breath or shouted "Oh my God!" anytime I drove the narrow streets of Italy's walled cities. It was fortunate, therefore, that we were both authorized drivers on each lease.

Another complicating factor with this lease program is that you have to pick up and drop off at the same location; otherwise, you incur a rather stiff penalty. Since we picked up our Citroen C4 Picasso at Munich's airport, that is where we had to drop it off and pick up the next C4 Picasso. As a result, we needed a good reason to return to Munich at some point in our travels, and Helga Eckart, our long time Munich friend, provided us the opportunity.

Helga was celebrating a significant (meaning large) birthday in June, and given that we were in Italy, she would have disowned us if we failed to attend. In addition, over the years we enjoyed numerous Munich Oktoberfests with Helga's two sons, so there was never any question about whether we would attend or not. We would be there. The added bonus was that the trip would give us the opportunity to return to one of our favorite places, Garmisch-Partenkirchen, which is nestled at the foothills of the Bavarian Alps and just a little over an hour drive south from Munich.

Earlier in the year when Helga announced her party, it was going to be in Pertisau, Austria, on Sunday, June 17. A few months later, she moved the party to Feldkirchen, Germany and the date to Sunday, June 24. This schedule change threw a wrinkle into our plans.

This change affected our travel plans with Theo and Heather, who had previously booked flights to visit us in Italy starting the Thursday after Helga's original birthday party date of June 17. While the four of us were in Greece, I had to break the news to Theo and Heather that instead of touring Italy with us, the four of us would be sightseeing in Germany.

On Thursday morning, we dropped Jack at his new pensione, headed to the Rome airport to pick up Theo and Heather from their flight from Athens, had a light lunch at the airport, and drove three hours north to a small town just north and east of Florence. Our stay in the Starhotels Vespucci in Campi Bisenzio was marginally satisfactory; however, dinner in the hotel restaurant was surprisingly good.

The next day we headed back through those 44 damn tunnels towards Bologna, through Austria, and then down to Garmisch-Partenkirchen. I started going to Garmisch-Partenkirchen in 1980 when I began work in Frankfurt. Since then, I have been back countless times and have a few favorite spots around the area that we frequent each time we return. One of our favorites is Café Panorama, which sits in the hills above Partenkirchen, and this was our first stop.

From this vantage point you can see Partenkirchen and then Garmisch in the valley below and right behind Garmisch are the Altspitze and the Zugspitze, the two tallest mountains in the Bavarian Alps. Sitting on the outdoor patio at this scenic location while breathing clean mountain air seems to make the beer and bratwurst taste so much better.

Just beyond Garmisch, about three miles closer to the Alps, is the town of Grainau, and in Grainau is the Alpenhof Hotel. It is not large or majestic; it is quaint, cozy, and beautifully decorated in traditional Bavarian style. The staff is super friendly and very accommodating. If in the Garmisch-Partenkirchen area and not consigned to a conference hotel, this is where I stayed. The hotel has a beautiful green space and at its rear an ice-cold mountain stream that adds to the relaxation factor.

The Alpenhof also has an amazing restaurant for a hotel its size. We dined there Friday evening to rave reviews from each of us. All the dinner plates at each table had cloches that were simultaneously removed by the restaurant staff to reveal the chef's artful displays. We were duly impressed when our meals were revealed. I had the pepper steak, Theo had my personal favorite, the wiener schnitzel (veal), Heather had the veal medallions in mushroom sauce, and Kathy had the pork tenderloin in cream sauce. I was the only glutton in the group and ordered my favorite German desert – vanilla ice cream with hot raspberries.

Saturday morning, David Eckart, Helga's oldest son and my Oktoberfest beer-drinking partner, joined us for breakfast, and then the five of us spent the day wandering the beautiful streets of downtown Garmisch. Nearly all of the buildings in Garmisch have hand painted scenes on their exteriors. Window flower boxes overflow with the most colorful varieties of the season. Most buildings have typical ski chalet style roofs with massive exterior wooden support beams. With a stream running through town, mountains surrounding the town for 270 degrees, and an abundance of outdoor dining venues, it is hard to find a more picturesque place on earth.

We walked a lot through these scenic towns not because we like to walk, which we truly don't mind, but because it assuaged some of our guilt about constantly eating and drinking. Spend a few calories walking here, enjoy a beer sitting there. After a few hours of wandering, we headed to Zum Wildschutz for a light lunch. We discovered this small restaurant on one of our trips. It offers a typical Bavarian menu but specializes in wild meats such as: pheasant, duck, deer and wild boar.

We followed the Greek style of dining and shared a variety of appetizer selections, which we washed down with Hacker-Pschorr beer, the same beer served at Café Panorama. Hacker-Pschorr is one of my favorites, along with Paulaner, Spaten, Lowenbrau, and every other Munich-brewed beer. Following lunch, we headed to the Riessersee, another must-see venue when visiting Garmisch.

The Riessersee is near the south end of Garmisch and nestled in the hills east of the town, in the same general direction as the Hausberg ski slopes. You take a serpentine road up approximately a mile to a mirror-like lake fed by melting ice and rain from the surrounding mountains. On the very north end of the lake sits a lone beautiful Gasthaus with an expansive outdoor dining area. On the south end of the lake, the stone and granite Altspitze, along with some of its lower elevation neighbors, rises up behind a forest of beautiful dark green pine trees.

The lake has the shape of an arrowhead with the point heading in the direction of the Altspitze. The walk around the lake is about three fourths of a mile and intersects with other trails that take you deeper into the hills. Sitting at the Gasthaus' outside seating area provides an amazing perspective. Since the trees mirror the shape of the lake, your eyes are drawn to the tip of the lake and then up to the magnificent gray glacial mountains. On a clear, sunny day, the image of the Altspitze is reflected in the waters of the Riessersee. With a beer or wine at your disposal, it becomes amazingly easy to slip into a transcendental state.

David was not able to spend the night with us in Grainau but agreed to join us for dinner before going back to Munich. Having been impressed with our previous night's meal at the Alpenhof, we elected to return there for dinner. David and I chose what Theo enjoyed the night before, the wiener schnitzel. Theo selected what Heather previously enjoyed, the veal medallions in mushroom gravy. Kathy chose grilled prawns, and Heather opted for a large salad. When the plates arrived, they were sans cloche. When we asked the waiter about this, he matter-of-factly said: "Oh, sorry. Friday is cloche night," and walked away. We all looked at one other and giggled.

On Sunday, Giselle took us for an hour and 15-minute drive through Bavaria's farmlands and forests to the Aschbacher Hof Hotel in Feldkirchen. The Aschbacher Hof is a German style country inn situated among beautiful rolling hills and with views of the distant mountains. We checked into our respective rooms and then joined Helga and family and friends for a two-hour reception followed by a delicious five-course dinner. It was a tough six hours of drinking and dining but we muddled through somehow.

Monday morning, Kathy and I went to the Munich airport to exchange Giselle I for Giselle II. With Giselle I, we covered over 4,400 kilometers, or about 2,600 miles, without incident; a few close calls heading to and from the Rome airport, but no dents, dings, or scratches. We signed for Giselle II, picked up Theo and Heather at the Aschbacher Hof, and headed for Verona where we would spend the night.

We arrived in Verona later that afternoon and checked into the Hotel Antica Porta Leona. Never stayed in a hotel with three names, but there is a first time for everything. I am not sure when the building was constructed or what it was before it became a hotel, but one thing I do know is that there are very few right angles anywhere in the hotel and very few room walls are the same length. It is disconcerting to be in rooms that are not square or rectangular. Regardless, this boutique hotel was delightfully furnished and the staff totally accommodating.

Theo wanted "great" pizza before heading back to Australia, which they would do on Wednesday, so I compiled a list of the top five pizza places in Verona. When I presented the list to one of the hotel clerks who professed to be a pizza guru, he immediately picked one of the five and then pointed out the window to Sapore Downtown Gourmet Pizza, less than 20 yards away. He was also kind enough to book a table for us. With a few hours to kill, we headed out to explore Verona.

We walked half a block from the narrow street where our hotel resided to Via Cappello and then headed right towards Piazza Erbe. Five short blocks later we were at Casa Giulietta (of Romeo and Juliet fame) where tourists mobbed the courtyard below Juliet's balcony. The fact that the courtyard was mobbed with 100 tourists taking pictures of a small stone balcony was bad enough, but the house was open to the public, and every few minutes some new idiot emerged onto the balcony and waved to the crowd, then turned his back and took a panoramic selfie of the adoring masses below. Can't believe I had to wait a whole hour for my turn.

Once at Piazza Erbe, we took a left onto Via Mazzini, the main shopping street in Verona, which also happens to be a pedestrian thoroughfare, and approximately 10 short blocks later arrived at the Arena – Verona's version of Rome's Colosseum. The Arena, which is an absolutely stunning structure, is a fully functional Roman coliseum that predates the one in Rome, and actually served as one of the models used in the design of Rome's Colosseum. Carmen, Aida, Turandot, Nabucco, and The Barber of Seville were some of the operas being performed in the Arena that summer. A large and beautiful piazza is to the west of the Arena, and around the piazza's perimeter are a dozen sidewalk restaurants. A truly magical setting.

With the two ladies drifting in and out of stores on Via Mazzini, the return trip to our hotel took a little longer, but we made our 7:30 reservation at Sapore. The restaurant has four pizza crusts: thick, thin, crispy, and extra crispy – and within each category are a significant number of set ingredient combinations. Sometimes, self-proclaimed gourmet pizza places are not that great. The pizza here was excellent. We also had a superb 2014 Chianti Classico from Ormanni Vineyards, which we agreed was worth tracking down. Happily, the vineyard turns out to be a couple of hours from our home base, Perugia.

Verona has a population of approximately 270,000, about 100,000 less than Bologna and more than Perugia. Given that we had just two and a half hours to wander Verona, we barely scratched the surface of what Verona had to offer. However, with that brief introduction, we all agreed that city's vibe made it a worthwhile return destination. While we would visit Bologna again if in the vicinity, we would make a concerted effort to revisit Verona, so much so that we were contemplating catching an opera at the Arena in the coming months.

Our drive the next day was about five hours: past Modena, past Bologna, through those damn 44 tunnels, past Florence, and finally, to the Rome airport. We spent the night at the Rome Airport Hilton, and had an enjoyable farewell dinner with Theo and Heather. The next morning, we dropped them off at the airport for their 20+ hour combined flights back to South Australia, and then headed, with fingers crossed, to Parco Cinofilo Umbro to retrieve our boy Jack.

Chapter Twelve

The Bureaucracy Strikes Again and Again and Again

Wednesday, June 27 to Saturday, July 7

Lord Byron is the first one to be credited with the saying, "Truth is stranger than fiction," or words to that effect. A little over 70 years later, Mark Twain echoed the same sentiment. Now, 121 years after Mark Twain's pronouncement, I had begun to appreciate the depth of his and Lord Byron's wisdom.

As you recall, when Giuseppe and I went to the Perugia Administrative Office several weeks ago, we received multiple forms, that when filled in, would attest to the fact that I was a resident of Perugia, forms which Giuseppe completed on my behalf prior to heading on vacation for two weeks. Before leaving the administrative office, we also scheduled a follow-up appointment for June 28, the day after Kathy and I returned from Helga's birthday celebration in Germany.

Along with the three completed forms, I was asked to return with proof of health insurance. Since Giuseppe was unavailable, Sofia, our part-time dog sitter, agreed to accompany me. We showed up at the appointed time with the completed forms, my European Union passport, my retired Army ID card, my Medicare ID card, and my Veterans Administration ID card. We met with the same lady as before and laid out everything on her desk. Sofia did a great job interpreting between the two of us.

We were at this office to prove that I was a resident of Perugia, while at the same time prove that I had U.S. medical insurance that was valid overseas. But once I prove that I am a resident of Perugia, both my wife and I become eligible for Italian health insurance. If I successfully prove that I am a resident of Perugia, which I am, then why is it necessary to prove that I have health insurance from the United States? Words like ironic, paradoxical, incongruous come to mind. Let's throw in tedious as well.

All appeared to be going well, until the lady, Emma was her name, looked at my Medicare card and could not find an expiration date. The expiration date on my Department of Defense ID card is "indefinite," the expiration date on my VA ID card is 2024, but there is no place on the Medicare ID card for an expiration date — only an effective date. I explained the mandatory "age 65 till death do us part" thing but it fell on deaf ears. I told Emma if she knew when I was going to die, we could pencil in the date. That didn't help my case.

We left the Perugia Administrative Office one data point shy of success. No problem, I would just go to Medicare.Gov and find a web page that explains why there is no expiration date on Medicare ID cards and show it to Emma. After two hours of surfing Medicare.Gov, I came up empty-handed, an exercise that turned out to be mission impossible. Over the next four days, I placed three calls to Medicare asking, "Where on your website does it explain why there is no expiration date on Medicare ID cards?" Apparently, no such written explanation exists.

Undaunted, I forged ahead with research on the Department of Defense and the Veterans Administration websites, and with a few pages from the Medicare website, I believed that I had enough propaganda on the validity of my health insurance to win the heart and mind of Emma. All I needed now was to get a "legal" translation done of the salient points on each document.

When Giuseppe and I were at the Polizia Nazionale information office, the helpful lady, Katherine, explained that for Kathy's appointment on July 24, during which she would need to submit two passport photographs and be finger printed, she should bring a "legal" translation of our marriage license. We could get a legal translation done by going to the Prefettura di Perugia at 157 Via Corso Cavour, all of which she was kind enough to write on a piece of paper.

Now back from his vacation Giuseppe and I, armed with all the appropriate web pages, my identification cards, and the marriage certification, drove to the closest legal parking area near our destination, ("parking" in Italy is a whole separate discussion) and then headed on foot to the office of the Prefettura just outside the walled part of Perugia's south side. By the looks of the cobwebs on the padlocked steel grid that guarded the wooden door, and by the compacted debris lodged between the steel grid and the door, I suspected that the door to 157 Via Corso Cavour had not been opened in years.

We rechecked Katherine's handwritten note. Indeed, we were where we were directed to be. We shook our heads in disbelief, and then Giuseppe got on his phone to do some detective work. Right church, wrong pew, a different block of Corso Cavour. Anyone, even the Polizia Nazionale, can make a mistake. Off we headed to the correct address.

The entrance to the Prefettura di Perugia is guarded by a large and very thick iron and wooden horse and carriage door, within which lies a smaller human door. You gain entry only by pleading your case to the intercom attached to the stone wall on the right. If your case has merit, then the magnetic lock to the human door clicks and the door swings open. No merit, then no click.

Whenever I would go on Google Translate and plug in a few English sentences, the corresponding Italian translation seemed to be about 30 percent longer. The same must be true for the spoken word. As Giuseppe approached the squawk box, which does not contain the latest audio technology, to explain the merits of our case, three other folks walked up for their turns. He seemed to be taking a really long time loudly explaining things to the stone wall. The folks in waiting, as well as passersby across the street, were getting to hear more of my life story than was necessary. I believe I saw them shaking their heads in disbelief.

I assumed our case had no merit because there was no click. As the next person started his loud dissertation, Giuseppe said, "We are at the wrong place." Excuse me? "This office only stamps translations as official. It does not actually do any translations." Excuse me? We had to go to the Procura di Perugia Office in a Piazza Partigiani, not too far from there. Back to the car we went, drove to the new location, parked, and headed on foot to the designated building.

Unlike the office of the Prefettura di Perugia, this office allows you to enter the building and speak in person to a human being, albeit one behind a 4x8 sheet of bulletproof plexiglass. If your case has merit, then you place all of your belongings on a scanner, and head through a metal detector, all of which happens under the watchful eye of a military police officer with a machine gun. If your case has no merit, you leave in a reasonable amount of time or run the risk of getting shot.

As you are looking at the bulletproof plexiglass, the clerk sits on the left, and at counter level in front of where she sits is a single, small cut in the plexiglass to allow the passing of paper files back and forth. The natural inclination is to appear directly in front of the clerk and stoop down to direct your voice to the opening in the hopes that she will hear you, agree with the merits of your plea, and reward you with a visitor's pass.

Once Giuseppe began to articulate the facts of our case, the clerk started to wave him off like someone trying to warn a landing airplane of impending danger, and pointed to the opposite bottom corner of the plexiglass. It took a few moments for both of us to realize that she was directing Giuseppe to a small microphone taped to the bottom right side of the glass. Stoop down right and talk, but look up high and left. It was farcical at best. Once she got the gist of our story, the clerk responded into a microphone connected to speakers mounted above the plexiglass. Now a dozen more strangers were privy to my situation.

When the conversation ended, we did not head toward the metal scanner with visitors' badges as I had hoped but towards the exit door. "I will explain outside," said Giuseppe, shaking his head. "They don't do translations in this office, they only stamp translations as official." Excuse me? According to the clerk, we needed to go to the city center, to the third floor of the Judicial Building, where court clerks would take care of our needs.

Spurred on by either stupidity or blind faith or belief, that as Alexander Pope stated, "hope springs eternal in the human breast," we headed on foot up several hundred steps to the center of Perugia and located the Judicial Building. It was apparent by words and deeds that Giuseppe was totally embarrassed by the misinformation gushing from his city's government offices. What was less apparent was that he was equally sorry for having rented his Villa Nuba apartment to such needy Americans.

The guards at the Judicial Building were less serious but no less professional than the previous guards. Successfully through the metal scanner, we surrendered our identification card/passport, received visitor badges, and headed to Room 5 on the third floor. The gentleman inside Room 5 was personable, professional, and, according to the sign on the outside wall, a doctor of some kind. I was hoping he was a doctor of clairvoyance so we would not have to regurgitate our story for the third time that day. No such luck.

Giuseppe began, and the story seemed to get longer with each utterance. I assumed, on top of the base story, he was recounting all the day's previous encounters. The conversation went back and forth. There was a lot of nodding on both sides of the desk. The doctor seemed empathetic, but I saw no indication that led me to believe he was about to say, "OK, show me what you need, and we will get it translated." Finally, Giuseppe said, "Let's talk in the hallway." OK. "They don't do translations in this office. They only stamp translations as official." Excuse me?

So, let me get this straight. We had to find our own translator to translate what we needed? "Yes." Then, the translator would show up on the third floor of the Judicial Building and attest to the fact that he or she did the translation, and that it was accurate? "Yes." And the good doctor in Room 5 would stamp the translation as legally sufficient? "Yes." But unless the good doctor was fluent in English, he would have no clue that the translation was valid or not? "Yes." And Emma would accept these documents as gospel? "We hope so." Ah.

During the two weeks that all this residency drama was slowly unfolding, we visited Dr. Massimo two more times about our boy Jack. When we picked Jack up from Parco Cinofilo Umbro, the rash had not worsened, just relocated in a somewhat milder form to different parts of the body. Jack endured another blood draw, and another cortisone shot, and I endured another bill for 85 Euro. The blood test showed that Jack's thyroid function was within normal limits, a concern the doctor developed during a previous visit, and that Cushing's Disease, something the doctor wanted to check for, was not a factor.

During the next two weeks, I had no choice but to proceed full speed ahead on both Jack's health issues and Kathy's residency issues, but it was with trepidation that I did so for who knows what the bureaucracy would throw at me next. On the bright side, Dave and Joan would arrive the next day, so we looked forward to lots of giggles to break the stress of dealing with dysfunctional bureaucrats and befuddled doctors.

CHAPTER THIRTEEN

SPOLETO AND ASSISI

SATURDAY, JULY 7 TO WEDNESDAY, JULY 11

Having been educated in a Catholic grade school, high school, and college, I was exposed to one of the biggest bureaucracies in the world. I am not being judgmental; just pointing out that the Catholic Church, like all large bureaucracies, has a well-defined hierarchical structure, clearly articulated and printed rules and regulations, and set policies and procedures for conducting business. For 18 years, bureaucracy was all I knew.

I then entered the U.S. Army where for 20 years my bureaucratic experiences continued. Following the Army, I spent seven years on the information technology side of state government. While the unit I initially led was quasi profit and loss, in that it was funded through a charge-back system to using agencies, it still operated inside a bureaucracy, although slightly different from the preceding two.

It was not until I joined an internet start-up that I began to understand what it meant to be an entrepreneur and what incredible risks entrepreneurs take to create a business. These high risk, high reward individuals place their own personal wealth and reputation on the line every day. From my experience, entrepreneurs are a different breed, who are drawn to others of the same ilk, all of whom universally appear to abhor bureaucratic ways.

You now understand my biases, but you also know why I appreciate Giuseppe Nuzzaci so much. His network of fellow entrepreneurs in Perugia was impressive. If I had a problem, he knew a guy or a gal who could help. As was the case when, after visiting three separate government agencies, we finally learned that we needed to get our own translator, Giuseppe knew a lady who could get the job done.

Alessandra Ripadimeana is a tour guide, interpreter, translator, and Jill of all trades for tourism and language. When we met on Saturday, I gave her the complete background so she could understand the context of our translation request. Alessandra echoed Giuseppe's sense of disbelief. I think she and Giuseppe were more frustrated with Perugia's government than I was. Alessandra left with 10 pages to translate, all of which were designed to prove that I had health insurance from the United States. The work would take her about three days to complete.

— § —

Dave and Joan arrived on Monday via train from the Rome airport. Giuseppe was kind enough to pick them up, which provided the three of them time to renew old acquaintances. To their credit, Dave and Joan stayed awake until shortly after 8:00 p.m. But, circadian rhythms being what they are, Dave and Joan were wide awake and full of laughter at 5:30 the next morning, much to the dismay of their host, who likes to rise at the crack of noon.

Dave and Joan are retired attorneys from Chicago. Given their occupation and their former work location, it is easy to guess on whose political team they play. Since I play on the opposing team, Joan was wise enough to declare Italy a politics free zone for the week. Sports, weather, food, wine, and religious discussions were allowed, and Joan was the enforcer. Such enforcement did not dampen the festive spirit. Dave and Joan are unstoppable when it comes to sightseeing, eating, and drinking. At the end of the week Kathy and I were exhausted, but it was a week filled with great experiences, outstanding meals, raucous laughter, and a few hiccups.

For the time period they were spending in Perugia, Dave and Joan had five main goals: visit Spoleto, revisit Assisi, visit Orvieto, spend time at the Umbria Jazz Fest, and figure out why Joan thought she had an oven during their previous two-week stay at Villa Nuba. By the end of the trip, we had achieved the first four goals. With a quick visit to the unit they rented at Villa Nuba, we completed the last goal. Joan's oven was actually a dishwasher. Oops.

On the evening of Dave and Joan's arrival, Kathy prepared a large antipasto salad, and fixed eggplant parmigiana in our DeLonghi counter-top convection/toaster oven. The meal was a big hit, and Joan appreciated learning the difference between a dishwasher and an oven. By the way, we donated the oven to Giuseppe as a thank you for the effort he expended on our behalf trying to get Jack healthy and Kathy legal.

Early Tuesday morning, after making sure all the neighbors knew we were alive and well, we walked to the patisserie and carted back a bag of croissants, which we enjoyed with coffee and fruit. Refueled and refreshed, we headed out to Spoleto with our boy Jack, or as the Italians liked to say, Jac-keh, in tow. Spoleto is about an hour drive from Villa Nuba, on the same route as Assisi, Spello, and Trevi, a small but delightful mountain top town.

We approached Spoleto from the south side and parked in the Spoletosfera parking garage. From there, we took a series of three successive underground escalators to the Piazza della Liberta, the point from which we began our walking tour. Had we parked on the west side at Posterna, we could have taken a series of a dozen escalators from the bottom of town to the fortress at the top of the hill that overlooks the town. The engineering it took to excavate under a medieval hilltop town, install thousands of yards of escalators, and not disrupt delicate architecture dating thousands of years is impressive.

I was disappointed to learn that Spoleto did not warrant space in Rick Steves' 2015 book on Italy. Spoleto is a truly enchanting hilltop town that hosts a dance and music festival each year during the first two weeks of July. Unfortunately, most entertainment starts late in the afternoon or early evening, so our early day visit was not conducive to catching any performances. Regardless, we had a special day in Spoleto.

Dave and Joan are not pretentious in any way. What you see is what you get. Joan is like an oaky and buttery chardonnay with hints of peach, pear, and apricot. One sip and you instantly want more. Dave is like a Brunello di Montalcino: gritty, earthy, complex. One sip and you are not sure if you want more, but decant the wine and let it breathe for a few hours, and the wine's exquisite character emerges.

I have gotten to appreciate Dave's personality and sense of humor over the years, and when he wanted to lead our group, I did not hesitate to relinquish my tour guide duties. As we made our way towards the town's highest point, Fortress Rocca Albornoziana, we stopped at the Piazza Del Duomo to visit the Cathedral di Santa Maria Assunta. From where we stood on Via A. Saffi, there was a wide pedestrian only street leading downhill to the U-shaped piazza at the end of which was a stage, and behind it was the Cathedral.

The piazza and the street were filled with chairs for an upcoming performance. From our vantage point, it was easy to imagine the street as the stem and the piazza as the bowl of a chalice with the Cathedral hovering as a host above the chalice. On both sides of the street and the piazza were majestic buildings whose windows and porches were filled with flower boxes. It was a magical amphitheater setting, and we bemoaned the fact that our timing did not allow attending a performance.

A block later, we reached the Piazza Campello, which lies just below the base of the fortress. The route up to the fortress was steep, winding, long, and somewhat torturous given the hot weather. Dave, Jack, and I, men that we are, met the challenge head-on and started our hike. The ladies chose a more feminine and brilliant solution. They walked downhill five blocks to an escalator station they had noticed earlier. Thinking they would reach the fortress the easy way, the escalator deposited them right back at Piazza Campello, a hundred yards from where they started.

After more wandering, we headed to Piazza della Liberta for lunch at Ristorante Sabatini Il Giardino del Corso, which had a beautiful outdoor seating area. Given our asparagus flan experience, we were on the lookout for dishes with which we were not familiar, and this restaurant had one: flan of black celery stuffed with soft cheese and black truffle. We were not courageous enough to order four, so we went with one to share, a decision we ruminated on for the rest of the day since the dish was so amazing. We headed home to console ourselves with more wine.

— § —

On Wednesday morning, the translator, Alessandra, and I met in front of the Justice Building, Piazza Matteotti, in Perugia's city center. Through security we went, and with visitor badges and translations in hand we proceeded to the third floor to see the good doctor in Room 5 who was intimately familiar with the background of my case. To my dismay, the doctor in Room 5 was not working that day, so we were directed to Room 4 to see another, hopefully good, doctor.

I am not sure how or in what discipline this lady earned her PhD. All I do know is that she earned it a very, very long time ago. She appeared to be in her late 70s, but was probably younger, with dyed jet black scraggly long hair, horn-rimmed glasses, and a sense of movement that could only be described as a pantomime in slow motion. There were numerous times that I wanted to reach across the desk and touch her because I thought she might have died in mid-sentence.

While Alessandra had to stay in the room to attest to her qualifications and the authenticity of her work, I had to depart to the closest tobacco store, yes tobacco store, to purchase 80 Euro worth of stick-on government tax stamps. When I returned, Alessandra and I engaged in a low-level conversation, only to be chastised by the matronly ex-teacher and warned that she might have to start over were we to continue the unnecessary interruption. We avoided a trip to the principal's office, and one excruciatingly slow-motion hour later, we departed with our stamped and certified document translations.

Kathy elected to give Dave, Joan, and me a Jack-free day, so late Wednesday morning the three of us headed to Assisi. Like Giselle I, Giselle II took us on the same tranquil route to the parking garage at Piazza Matteotti, high above the city center. With Rick Steves' walking guide in hand, Dave led us on a masterfully narrated exploration of Assisi and all things St. Francis. Having not entered a single building on my first visit, on this trip I was totally absorbed by all we experienced.

The Cathedral of San Rufino, the Temple of Minerva, and the Basilica of St. Clare were impressive, but my favorite structure inside the walls of Assisi was the Lower Basilica of St. Francis. The Upper Basilica is indeed impressive, but the frescoes and mosaic designs on every portion of the Lower Basilica were mind blowing, and the presence of the tomb of St. Francis made the visit to this memorial truly significant.

While our trip to Assisi was not gastronomically focused, I would be remiss to omit the fact that we dined at a delightful restaurant, and one that I would willingly revisit, called Osteria Piazzetta Dell'Erba.

Our tour guide continued his superb job and, after a few more strategic stops, Dave artfully led us back to the parking garage at Piazza Matteotti, where yours truly discovered he had lost the parking ticket, an action for which I received extensive verbal abuse from my two travel companions.

The vast majority of Italy's fee-based parking structures are unmanned. No ticket? No car. Since all the pay station instructions are in Italian, it took some time to determine which button to push to contact a human being. With broken English and broken Italian, it took four successive phone conversations for the privilege of paying double the going rate to retrieve Giselle, an action accompanied by more verbal abuse from my travel companions. The patrons behind us waiting to retrieve their vehicles were not amused by our antics.

Departing Assisi, we headed for the valley below to the Church of Santa Maria Degli Angeli, a structure that Dave and Joan kept calling the church within the church, which I failed to comprehend fully. According to some references I checked, Santa Maria Degli Angeli is the seventh largest Catholic church in the world. When we entered the church, we could see what looked like a shed for a nativity scene perhaps three fourths of the way up the main aisle.

When we reached the "shed," everything came into focus. Once I realized what was in front of me, I felt like I had been hit with a ton of bricks. I was standing by the original church of St. Francis of Assisi over which was built this massive Basilica. Inside the tiny church of St. Francis was a Franciscan priest reciting the rosary out loud, accompanied by perhaps 30 fellow Christians. The significance of what I was viewing moved me to tears.

PICTURES

PART I

TIME TO USE YOUR IMAGINATION.

Create Space/Kindle Direct Publishing on Amazon.Com gives authors two mutually exclusive printing choices when self-publishing. Print in black and white or print in color. Printing in color would have raised the cost of this book by five hundred percent. Therefore, the following pictures, and those in Part II, are in black and white, not in their original color. If so moved, feel free to color the pictures. It is OK to color outside the lines.

Jack at 14 weeks of age soaking up the sun in our
South Carolina driveway

Hello to Giselle I - which we drove for 4,488 kilometers

Hotel Villa Giona in San Pietro in Cariano

The courtyard at Hotel Villa Giona

One of the buildings at Villa Nuba Apartments. We occupied
the two-bedroom unit on the ground level of this building

Our home away from home for six months

Giuseppe Nuzzaci, our landlord at Villa Nuba

Doctor Massimo Crecco and wife Simona with Jack

Lunch is about to be served in Thessaloniki

A waterside lunch at the Gondola restaurant in Perea - not too far from Thessaloniki

The large five-piece antipasto platter Kathy purchased from
Stefania's Ceramic Shop in Castiglione Del Lago on Lake
Trasimeno

Nicoletta and Chef Claudio with Giuseppe at La
Taverna Ristorante

Chapter Fourteen

The Dave Factor

Thursday, July 12 to Saturday, July 14

I dropped Jack off at his countryside retreat, Parco Cinofilo Umbro, because we planned on spending the day in Orvieto with Dave and Joan. The day before the last visit to this pensione, Jack received a dosage of Bayer Advocate liquid solution on his neck and upper back. Now three weeks later, his skin was looking better than it had since our arrival.

In the hope of maintaining Jack's improving appearance, I would need to apply a new dose of the same solution to Jack's back on the 16th of July. While we had no definitive cause for the rash yet, or which approach was having the greatest impact, we were just happy that Jack appeared to be on the road to normal skin.

— § —

When I arrived back at Villa Nuba from the pensione to retrieve Kathy and our guests for the trip to Orvieto, Dave informed me that there was a change in plans. Instead of going directly to Orvieto, we would be stopping first at Civita di Bagnoregio, which according to Dave, is Rick Steves' favorite hilltop town in Umbria.

Civita di Bagnoregio is a pedestrian only small town perched precariously on top of a vertical rocky stalagmite looking hill. The town is pedestrian only because there is just one way to reach the town, and that is via an elevated and steep pedestrian walkway that stretches across the valley between the town of Civita and the town of Bagnoregio.

Since Dave was now the tour-guide-du-jour, I requested only an address to provide Giselle. Dave assured me that he had the parking lot address locked in, and he had an address for the best lunch place in Civita. Armed with those two addresses, I was confident Giselle and I would be able to get us there. The rest would be up to Dave.

The route from Perugia to Orvieto is a reasonably straight forward hour and 25-minute drive. The route to Civita di Bagnoregio, which sits about 30 minutes south and a little west of Orvieto, is a little more convoluted. We followed the

E45/SS3bis, a ragged four-lane highway out of town south past Deruta, then near the town of Todi, about the half-way point, we headed southwest on a two-lane winding and hilly road towards our selected parking site.

The bad news is that immediately after making the turn, we found ourselves in a line of cars behind a very large gravel truck apparently heading to Orvieto at a snail's pace, so the 15-minute drive to the side road that would lead us to Civita di Bagnoregio turned into 40 minutes. The good news is that, with somewhat frazzled nerves, we arrived at our parking lot only 25 minutes behind schedule, and had no trouble finding a space for Giselle.

We had no trouble because we were the only car in the parking lot, which was really not a parking lot but a side street with painted blue lines near some empty fields somewhere on the outskirts of Bagnoregio, with no sign of any hilltop town, or town of any kind, on the horizon. Well, Dave? After some general crankiness, well-deserved finger pointing, and frantic googling, we decided to enter the address for Dave's restaurant inside the pedestrian town of Civita. My lost parking ticket during our Assisi trip was now looking more like a misdemeanor than the felony Dave and Joan made it appear to be.

After driving around Bagnoregio, we finally passed through an ancient archway with signs pointing to the medieval town of Civita. According to Giselle, the restaurant in Civita was only 400 meters away, and since we knew not what lay ahead, and since there was a parking spot by the arch, we elected to leave Giselle there.

Four hundred meters later, there was no sign of the hilltop town of Civita, let alone Dave's restaurant. Dave and I stopped by a lady merchant standing in her shop's doorway and asked, "This is Civita, correct?"

"No, this is Bagnoregio."

"So, what town is on the far side of the old archway through which we just entered?"

"That's the new part of Bagnoregio."

"So, where is Civita?"

"About 3,000 meters straight ahead."

Well, Dave?

The walk to the far edge of Bagnoregio was long but exhilarating. From there, the view of Civita perched in the distance was spectacular. The hike down to the pedestrian walkway and the hike up to Civita was stunning but taxing. The town was delightful, and the lunch at Alma Civita Ristorante, accompanied by a bottle of Orvieto's white grape "Liquid Gold" wine, was superb.

Our parking permit was 25 minutes away from expiring, and not wanting to be stranded without Giselle, we force-marched back to our starting point, and, with the air conditioning on full blast, headed to Orvieto. Luckily, we found a parking space in a lot not too far from the Duomo, and with the help of some locals, arrived on foot at our destination without making any wrong turns.

My experience has been that the simpler the outside of a cathedral or basilica, the more ornate the inside tends to be, and vice versa. This was the case here. The outside of the Duomo Di Orvieto was described in Rick Steves' guidebook as "Italy's liveliest façade – a medieval altarpiece." Highly ornate gothic architecture, four exquisite spires, mosaic inlays, and massive doors made the Duomo one of the most beautiful I have seen. The interior, while not plain, could not compare to the Lower Basilica of Assisi and other plain-faced cathedrals we have visited.

With a dinner reservation at La Taverna that evening, having expended a significant amount of energy finding and visiting Civita di Bagnoregio, and being behind schedule, we cut our time in Orvieto short, a disservice to this beautiful medieval hilltop town.

Giuseppe Nuzzaci joined us for dinner at La Taverna, one of the many places throughout Perugia where the Villa Nuba Gold Card will get you a discount. Giuseppe and Claudio, La Taverna's owner and executive chef, are long-time friends, and since Giuseppe had not dined there in some time, it gave them a chance to catch up. In addition, we learned that Giuseppe's divorce agreement, while not yet legal, was blessed by all parties involved, so we had one more reason to celebrate.

As always, dinner was phenomenal and the service superb. Shortly before the dinner service started, Josie, the host who first welcomed us to La Taverna, stopped by the table to say hello. As we were introducing our fellow diners, Giuseppe got up and gave Josie a big hug. It turned out that he and Josie were childhood friends. In fact, he considered Josie a big brother since Josie, a former Brazilian kick boxer, protected Giuseppe from neighborhood bullies during their adolescent years. A small world indeed, and another reason to celebrate.

With our friends in town, Giuseppe's divorce on track, and old acquaintances being renewed, the conversation and wine flowed freely, perhaps too freely. During this magical evening, the conversation naturally turned to the Umbria

Jazz Fest, which was set to start the next day, and was the main reason Dave and Joan came to Italy.

During the Jazz Fest conversation, Giuseppe shared the fact that years ago his father was with the Umbria Tourism Bureau, and he and another worker conceived the Jazz Fest idea, sold the concept, implemented the plan for the first Jazz Fest, and managed the Fest, now 45 years old, for a number of years. Umbria Jazz Fest royalty in our midst. Another reason to celebrate. Limoncello for the table!

There was not a lot of rising and shining come Friday morning. Subdued exuberance was the order of the day. After easing into the morning and clearing out some cobwebs, we headed out for Deruta, the ceramic capital of Italy. There is nothing like visiting store after store after store with thousands of gaudy, dizzying, mismatched plate patterns to sober one up. The Houlihans left unscathed; Dave and Joan bought Limoncello cups. Time for lunch and rehabilitative wine.

The sales lady at the last store we visited recommended a restaurant called "Siro" in Torgiano, about eight kilometers from Deruta on the way towards Perugia, which she claimed was the best restaurant in the area. The appetizer of grilled goat cheese with sliced apple and honey was divine. The rest of the courses were equally superb. We added Ristorante Siro to a growing list of places to which we want to return.

Another reason Dave and Joan came to Italy was so that Joan, an unabashed opera buff, could attend Puccini's opera *Tosca*, which was being performed in Puccini's home town, Torre Del Lago-Puccini, about 20 miles north of Pisa. To that end, they rented a two bedroom Airbnb on a mountain top, about eight miles north and east of the opera venue. They invited us to join them at their villa, our final destination on Saturday. Since Friday was their last day in Perugia, after pool time, nap time, and light snacks, Dave, Joan, and Dan headed to Jazz Fest. Kathy, the wise one, stayed home and rested up for the early morning departure to Volterra and points north, a combined four-hour drive.

Volterra, a favorite of ours from a previous trip to Tuscany, is more a working town than a tourist town, though it gets its fair share of guests. I contracted with Arianna & Friends for a walking tour of Volterra. Our guide, Monika, did a wonderful job balancing history, architecture, and culture into her presentation. The once hidden Roman baths and arena ruins were the highlight of the trip. From there we had wine tasting and lunch at La Spinetta in Terricciola. Although we tasted about eight wines, my discerning pallet apparently was on strike from over stimulation.

Dave and Joan's villa was on the outskirts of a small village called Piano Di Mommio. None, and I mean none, of the available map applications could find the address, leading us to understand why the emailed instructions on finding the villa seemed so mysterious. We were able to find an address on the street right before the digital map turned blank, so we plugged the address into Giselle. We knew that the next street would be the start point of our villa search.

Giselle guided us through the extremely narrow streets of Piano Di Mommio to our programmed destination. From there, the first search clue was that there would be a narrow open gate, so we proceeded cautiously and after one block, we found such gate leading to a dark and foreboding forested area.

Parked outside the gate was a small white sedan, and standing next to the sedan was a woman with papers in her hand. As soon as she saw our car, she smiled and started waving at us. Dave rolled down his window and said, "You must be Silvia?"

"No, I am Sophia, but I am here to guide you to your villa. Just follow me." How psychic of her to know when we would arrive.

We passed through the narrow gate, and 50 yards later the extremely narrow single lane road took an incredibly sharp left turn and proceeded uphill at about a 40-degree angle. For the next mile and a half, we proceeded at a snail's pace up this dizzying vertical road alternating between one sharp switch back after another. If the tree roots popping up the pavement were not enough to slow you down, the pot holes certainly were.

To add insult to injury, the residents whose homes were hard to spy through the overgrown vine and tree canopy, added speed bumps and posted speed signs. If that were not enough, the proximity warning indicators on Giselle's front and rear bumpers were constantly beeping just in case I failed to notice how narrow the road was. And oncoming traffic? Someone would have to back uphill or downhill to find a gap in the trees, or one of the few driveways, or one of the fewer spots on the road wide enough to allow the other car to pass.

Having already been driving for four hours, and having survived this vertical version of Deliverance, when we arrived at our destination I was not the happiest camper in the world. I was selfishly determined to make as few trips on this road as possible. Dave and Joan went inside to check things out while Kathy and I started unloading. After a while, Dave came out and said, "This isn't our house. We are at the wrong house. She thought we were a family from Germany."

Well, Dave?

CHAPTER FIFTEEN

THE DAVE FACTOR, PART II; THE BUREAUCRACY STRIKES AGAIN

SATURDAY, JULY 14 TO WEDNESDAY JULY 25

You can't be serious, Dave. This is not your villa?

While I was trying to figure out whether to scream or cry (laughter was not one of the options available), Dave and Joan scrambled through their notes for a telephone number so they could call the right version of Silvia, and they succeeded. Shortly thereafter, Silvia's husband showed up on a scooter, local knowledge trumps unsuspecting tourists in cars, and he escorted us 100 yards ------ -- to the house next door.

Mr. Mixed Emotions struck again. I was joyous at the thought that we would not have to drive back down and restart our villa search. Then, terrified by the prospect that every time we needed to go anywhere for anything, we would have to drive the same treacherous route. While I was publicly pouting, Dave, who I think was equally perplexed but less demonstrative about it, was trying to process the fact that none of the previous villa guests mentioned the torturous drive in their reviews.

Meanwhile, Joan and Kathy kept their composure. At Joan's suggestion, Dave and I, with shopping list in hand, made a trip down and back, to the only grocery store in Piano di Mommio to gather provisions to get us through the evening. We accomplished the mission with limited conversation. On our return, Dave's constant humorous cajoling and the sound of a cork leaving a wine bottle finally got me out of my funk. At which time, I was quick to point out that, in retrospect, my lost parking ticket was now looking pretty insignificant.

The cozy, two-bedroom villa, which had delightful grounds and swimming pool, provided amazing views of Pisa and the Ligurian Sea in the distance. The next day, Joan and I made a trip for breakfast pastries and lunch provisions. Then I made a solo trip to town because I forgot an item while on the previous trip. While these trips were no shorter or easier, they were less terrifying because I now knew what was around every turn, and I was continually hoping that around each narrow turn I wouldn't encounter an oncoming car. No such luck.

Kathy and I are not "opera goers," but the thought of being in Puccini's home town during the annual Puccini Festival and witnessing one of his more popular operas in an open-air theater accompanied by two friends and ardent *Tosca* fans was compelling. Dave had previously printed out Act I of *Tosca*, and during the trip from Perugia to Pisa graced us with his animated narration, while Joan added appropriate background and color commentary on Act I, and then they both synthesized Acts II and III. We were armed and educated for what lay ahead.

Given the late hour at which the opera was projected to end, close to 1:00 a.m., and not wanting to risk life and limb and Giselle returning to the villa, we elected to overnight near the opera venue. This plan allowed us to enjoy a leisurely afternoon by the villa pool, head to town and change clothes in our hotel, watch the World Cup finale, then enjoy a wonderful dinner at Ristorante La Limonaia.

When the tables fill up quickly after the restaurant opens, and you are the only strangers in the place, you know you found someplace special. La Limonaia was this kind of place. The meals were superb with Joan's "spaghetti con frutti di mare" leading the way, as attested to by her Meg Ryan imitation. To cap things off, we have found La Limonaia is one of the few Italian restaurants that keeps its Limoncello and the Limoncello glasses in the freezer. Grazie.

The weather cooperated, the opera kicked off around 9:30 p.m., and, thanks to Dave and Joan's setting the "stage," we had a most wonderful *Tosca* experience. Being center aisle, rows 13 and 14, enhanced the experience. We knew when to yell Brava and Bravo and when to boo and when to cheer – which didn't happen much since this was an Italian opera and everyone dies before it's all over.

Dave and Joan were spending an additional week in Piano di Mommio and needed to pick up a rental car in Pisa. So, on Monday late morning we dropped them off at Europcar in Pisa and headed to home base Perugia to retrieve our boy Jack.

Jack was in good spirits when we picked him up, and his rash looked like it was continuing to clear up. That evening, I applied a second dose of Advantix Advocate to his neck and upper back.

Two days later, we were dining outdoors at Il Pettirosso, and the table cloth corner waving in the breeze was too much of a temptation for Jack. The fastest mouth in the west snagged the corner and gave the tablecloth a tug. Down on his head, neck, and upper back came a full glass of Sangiovese. If the rash immediately cleared up, I was not going to be too happy about having to share my Sangiovese with Jack.

— § —

On Tuesday morning, Giuseppe and I headed to see Emma at the Perugia Administrative Office – my third trip and Giuseppe's second. We were about fourth in line, and Emma was behind Desk 3 in the open bay, instead of in her normal office. While waiting our turn, Giuseppe peeked in one of the other offices and came back all smiles. "I know the lady in that office. She used to be my neighbor. And I think that she is the supervisor of the office."

The animated conversation that Giuseppe and the supervisor had within Emma's line of sight was not lost on Emma. Giuseppe reinforced the neighborly connection once we sat down. I expected Emma to scrutinize my 10 pages of documents and their stamped and certified translations. But she didn't. She just scanned through them while Giuseppe was updating her on our efforts since the last visit. She went to her computer, printed out a page, signed and stamped it, and gave me a form that said my residency application was officially submitted, and final approval would be sometime after her supervisor reviewed the file.

Apparently, we caught Emma in a good mood, because as Giuseppe was going over the checklist of things we needed for the big meeting at the Polizia Nazionale, she offered to help. Emma volunteered to complete one of the forms on our behalf, and then called a different Perugia government office to process the remainder, which she projected would be ready by Friday or Monday at the latest. Her help cost me 32 Euro more in tax stamps.

On Friday, Giuseppe, who was out of town, texted me to say that the rest of the documents were ready, so early Monday morning I headed to this other administrative office, signed three forms and received four documents. After running a few errands, I returned to Villa Nuba to find an officer of the Polizia Nazionale waiting to meet with the owners of Villa Nuba and with me. Fortunately, Giuseppe's parents were available.

After questioning Mr. and Mrs. Nuzzaci about the property and apparently about me, my best guess since all conversations transpired in Italian, the officer took pictures of my passport, the apartment rental agreement, and a couple of other forms with her cell phone. Mr. Nuzzaci indicated, as best he could with severely limited English, that my residency application submission process was complete. With our big meeting at the Polizia Nazionale tomorrow, timing could not have been better.

Monday afternoon I found a copy shop where I could make copies of passports, visa stamps, and the pages I had received from Perugia's administrative office. Since we would be heading to the police station without an interpreter, I crafted a paper explaining all the necessary background and used Google Translate to convert it to Italian. Kathy got her four passport photos for 5 Euro at a passport photo machine, and I purchased 32 Euro more of tax stamps needed for the residency card application. Since Wednesday would be our 90th day in the European Union, I believed we had everything so Kathy's stay beyond 90 days would be legal.

We arrived at Polizia Nazionale 10 minutes before our morning appointment time. As it turned out, the appointment time was a joke. When we arrived, there was a line of 10 folks already waiting to enter through the police gate. The gate opened just as we were crossing the street, so we ended up in a queue for the clerk behind the plexiglass at Window 1. After about 10 minutes, a second clerk arrived at Window 2, and when it was our turn, she became our clerk.

As she read my introduction, she started making unpleasant faces and shaking her head side to side. I took that as an indication that this might be a long day. She spoke limited English, and when I failed to understand what she was asking for next, she became agitated. When she finally had the papers she was requesting, she started leafing through them and mumbling the word "No," over and over again. Finally, she moved all our papers to Window 3 and told us that we would have to wait for her English-speaking colleague to come to work.

Thirty minutes later, the English-speaking colleague arrived, and I proceeded to educate her on our saga. She listened and then conferred with her colleague. The issues were two. The fact that I had completed all the steps for my residency application was meaningless to clerk Number 2; she needed the final approval of my residency. Her position was the opposite of what Katherina in the police information office told us back in late May. According to Katherina, since a residency application approval can take several months, "All we need to move forward with your wife's residency card is for you to complete your residency application."

The second issue revolved around the copy of our marriage record, two copies of which Kathy received a few weeks prior to our departure. The fact that the raised seal of the Clerk of the Circuit Court of Marion County, Indianapolis, Indiana was on the certificate, and the certificate was translated and attested to by the Perugia Judicial Tribunal was inconsequential. They needed an "Apostille" certified copy. Neither of these two issues was ever mentioned by the clerk behind Window 3 at the Italian Consulate in Coral Gables, Florida.

Around and around we went. Another co-worker became involved. When I brought up the concern of going through passport control in Munich and their system would highlight the fact that Kathy overstayed her visa by 100 plus days, the answer I received was, "They won't care. You are leaving the country." So, what if they did care? Her passport could be flagged and she could be barred from re-entering the entire Schengen area of the European Union. "Then show them your marriage certificate." The same marriage certificate that you won't accept as legally sufficient?

While they offered a Band-Aid solution, we failed to reach a legally sufficient compromise, so we left empty-handed. Effective the next day, Kathy would be in Europe illegally. As we were leaving the office, I thought that it was probably not a good time to mention that I also needed their help because I did not have an international driving permit for Italy and had been driving here illegally for three months. Better to ask for forgiveness later than to ask for permission now?

Giuseppe returned from vacation the following day, and I went over the details of our meeting with the Polizia Nazionale. It took a while for me to calm him down. Per Giuseppe, we were heading back to the police station verbal guns a-blazing.

Chapter Sixteen

Polizia Nazionale

Wednesday July 25 to Monday, July 30

On Thursday morning, Giuseppe and I headed to the Polizia Nazionale. Since Giuseppe had done all the talking on our previous visits there, he was particularly upset about the differing opinions concerning my residency application submission being "completed" versus the application being "approved." Giuseppe was armed and loquacious when we arrived and wasted no time firing verbal bullets.

Our first meeting was with Katherina in the information office. She was the one who initially assured us that all we needed to do was complete the application process for my residency, and then the police could go ahead and process Kathy's residency card. After a 10-minute Italian conversation, the best I could determine was that Katherina still espoused the "submission completed" policy and was dumbfounded by her co-worker's "submission approved" policy. We left her one-person office, much to the dismay of the queue of folks lined up awaiting their turn, and headed to a supervisor's office next door.

The lady next door turned out to be the English-speaking associate Kathy and I met with two days earlier. While Katherina was in her late 30s and wore a police uniform, the supervisor did not appear to be a uniformed officer. She was in her mid-50s with scraggly dark hair, large glasses, a slow-talking deep voice, and Jack Benny like mannerisms.

Had it not been for the seriousness of the issue, the interactions of the three could be described as comical. They looked like dysfunctional family members arguing over whose turn it was to do the dishes. Sometimes they spoke individually, but more often all three were talking at the same time with hands and arms waving to emphasize a point.

While the office door was slightly ajar at the start of the meeting, I closed the door as the volume and intensity of the conversations increased. Since the office had no ceiling, closing the door was ineffective, and the dozen people in the bay area waiting for the clerks behind bulletproof plexiglass were privy to our situation.

Katherina returned to her office to tend to her line of customers, while Giuseppe and Jack Benny continued to talk in Italian. I had been silent to this point, but during a pause in the conversation interjected that we were following the guidance of the Italian Consulate in Coral Gables, Florida, and I was still concerned that upon departure, without a residency card, Kathy's passport could be flagged, and she could be barred from re-entering the EU.

With a Jack Benny-like hand and arm gesture, she said: "Well, I travel a lot, and I assure you that since you are leaving the country, they won't care how long you have been here."

"And if they do care?"

Giuseppe and Jack Benny continued speaking in Italian. After a short while, we exited the office and approached the head-shaking, face-making clerk from two days ago behind Window 2. The two associates consulted and decided to go see their boss. They asked us to wait in the bay area.

While waiting, Giuseppe told me that Katherina was misinformed, and, therefore, misinformed us about my residency application. According to the supervisor, the policy changed over a year ago, and now residency "approval" was required. I sensed that the Polizia Nazionale associates were a little embarrassed and would at least try to reach some accommodation. After 10 minutes, they called us back to an office behind the bulletproof service windows.

The Italian dialog continued for another 20 minutes, with the supervisor's supervisor coming in at one point. Since it appeared that further discussion of my residency submission versus approval was pointless, the conversation eventually turned to our marriage certificate, and the fact that the certificate needed to be an Apostille certificate. Giuseppe tried to explain the requirement, which I failed to fully appreciate. They recommended that I consider going to the U.S. Embassy in Rome with our current marriage certificate and have the Embassy do an Apostille certification and translation.

I told them that we were going to Rome on Monday because we were flying to Dublin on Tuesday, and I would call this afternoon to see if the Embassy offered the service. Dead silence. It was as if I had just said some magic word. The two associates looked at each other, then the English-speaking supervisor, who twice previously said – "they won't care because you are leaving the country" – blurted: "That could be a problem because at this point your wife is no longer here legally." You can't be serious!

Twenty more minutes of dialogue ensued with Giuseppe masterfully orchestrating the process. They pulled regulations from the bookcase, and scratched their heads. Finally, the clerk from Window 2 agreed to start Kathy's formal application process for her residency card, and we would be provided proof of such, in case police of any kind stopped us during our last three months of travel. To do so, she needed Kathy at her office within the hour. The clerk further advised that Kathy's actual residency card issuance would only come with my residency approval and an Apostille marriage certificate.

I called my formally documented, now totally undocumented, illegal immigrant, criminal wife and let her know what was afoot. Giuseppe and I headed back to Villa Nuba where I collected Jack and Kathy and returned to the Polizia Nazionale office with 10 minutes to spare.

We provided passports and passport photos and our file of documents and watched the clerk at Window 2 bang on her computer, shuffle papers, cut pictures, and staple documents. We were directed to the fingerprint office, where Kathy was finger, palm, and hand printed, and then returned to Window 2. Upon our return, both window clerks stopped what they were doing and came out from behind the bulletproof glass to say hello and pet Jack (seriously). Then, the Window 2 clerk provided us with our copy of the formal Carta Di Soggiorno application, with Kathy's photo, signatures, and stamps in all the right places. Fingers crossed.

The next task was to procure an Apostille certification for our marriage certificate. While I had seen and heard the term Apostille, I was unfamiliar with its origin and use. Upon further research, I learned, thanks to Wikipedia, that:

"The Apostille Convention, or the Apostille Treaty, is an international treaty drafted by The Hague Conference on Private International Law. It specifies the modalities through which a document issued in one of the signatory countries can be certified for legal purposes in all the other signatory states. A certification under the terms of the convention is called an apostille (from Latin post illa and then French: a marginal note). It is an international certification comparable to a notarisation in domestic law, and normally supplements a local notarisation of the document. If the convention applies between two countries, such an apostille is sufficient to certify a document's validity, and removes the need for double-certification, by the originating country and then by the receiving country."

So, there you go.

— § —

While our consulates and embassies overseas provide wonderful services, speaking to a human being is not one of them. After failed calls and extensive online research, I determined that the American Embassy in Rome did not provide Apostille certification for marriage certificates. Now what?

Time for a segue. Kathy's sister Christine lives in a suburb of Indianapolis, Fishers to be exact, and is married to Dave, who is a retired Army colonel. Indianapolis, as it happens, is the location where Kathy and I were married. On further research, I learned that the secretary of state in each of our 50 states is authorized to issue Apostille documents, and the Indiana Secretary of State's office is located in Indianapolis, the state capital.

So, armed with this new information, I called brother-in-law Dave, not to be confused with the Dave of Joan and Dave oven fame. Although retired from the Army, brother-in-law Dave has a full-time job in Indianapolis, and I explained our dilemma to him. He committed to calling both the clerk of the court and the office of the secretary of state to see what he could find out.

Active and retired military have this incredible "can do" attitude: no mountain too high, no river too wide, accomplish the mission at all costs mentality. In less than two hours, Dave sent me a text from Indianapolis, advising me that he had procured two certified copies of our marriage record from the Clerk of the Marion County Circuit Court, and that he was on his way to the secretary of state's office. Approximately 90 minutes later, Dave sent another text containing one word - "Goal!" Dave dropped everything, at what cost I do not know, and hustled around Indianapolis to get us two Apostille certified copies of our marriage record. Incredible.

— § —

Dave and Christine's son Frank (Francis Amadeo-named after St. Francis of Assisi no less) is pretty bright. He is so bright that he graduated summa cum laude from his high school and received multiple college acceptance letters. To celebrate his achievements, Frank elected to visit Dublin, Ireland, as his graduation gift. Now that's what I call one really smart Italian.

Upon hearing this, we were not about to let Frank enjoy Dublin without us, so we booked flights to coincide with Frank's itinerary. As it turned out, we planned to meet Frank in Dublin on Wednesday, and with him, thanks to his father, would be two Apostille certified copies of our marriage record. Timing may not be everything, but it is sure nice when it works in your favor.

A few years ago, I bought a book titled *Unbroken* by Laura Hillenbrand, which was about the life of World War II veteran Louis Zamperini. For a variety of reasons, I had failed to get around to reading the book. Now that I was in Italy and not watching television, I caught up on my reading, and this week I finally read *Unbroken*. The point, you ask?

Over the past 90 days, we have been frustrated and agitated and disappointed with our constant battles with the Italian bureaucracy and with the misinformation from the Italian Consulate in the United States. In the big picture, though, our outrage is really small stuff. As a friend of mine used to say, "Worrying about this is like pole vaulting over mouse turds."

Compared to Louis Zamperini's ordeal, what we went through for Kathy's residency card is really small stuff. Those of you who have read the book about what Louis Zamperini endured while lost at sea for 46 days, and what he endured for two years in a series of Japanese POW camps, know exactly what I mean. To those not familiar with *Unbroken*, I highly recommend reading it.

Next up for us was a week holiday in Dublin. To ease the drama of Jack's health issues and the pain of dealing with the Polizia Nazionale, I suspected there might be a Guinness or a Jameson in our future. Perhaps, two.

Chapter Seventeen

"In Dublin's Fair City..."

Monday, July 30 to Wednesday, August 8

Monday, July 30 was the half-way point of our adventures in Europe. From this date forward, as they say, it was all downhill. On Monday, we dropped Jack at his pensione on our way to the Rome Airport Hilton. By the way, Jack's rash had been completely gone for about two weeks. We still did not know what caused the rash or which treatment cleared up the condition, but we remained hopeful it would not reappear.

The ride to Jack's pensione was about 25 minutes long, and for most of the ride Jack would lie on the back seat, oblivious to the passing landscape. Once we got on the gravel road to the pensione, he sat up, perked up his ears, and got very antsy. When I opened the door this time, I did not have a firm grip on his leash, and Jack bounded out of the car and raced 30 yards to Ilaria, the lady who works her magic with the dogs. "But Jack, we won't see you for nine days!" He never looked back. Tail wagging and butt wiggling, he just walked off with her, appearing never to give us a second thought. "But Jack, after all we have done for you...?"

— § —

Flying around Europe in July or August is really not a smart thing to do. Flying out of the Rome airport in July or August is really, really not a smart thing to do. The airport likes to play the game "hide your departure check-in counter location." Unlike most large U.S. airports, in Rome there are no set check-in counter locations for each airline. The locations float each day based on the number of flights scheduled and departure times. With all the international carriers, and all the European country sponsored carriers, and all the intra-Europe discount carriers, Rome's airport has 400 possible check-in counter locations.

The departure check-in terminal is murderously long. The check-in counters are arranged in a contiguous line of inverted U-shaped areas from one end of the terminal to the other. Each U-shaped area has about 15 check-in counters along each side. The result is that you have thousands of people and all their luggage milling around a few screens trying to figure out where to check in. When the locations are posted, a massive traffic jam ensues as folks make a mad dash to be first in line at their respective counter.

Showing up early, as we did, appeared to be of little value. Initially, our check-in counter was 315. I retrieved Kathy and our luggage, and as we were making our way to 315, I double checked the screen and saw we were then to go to check-in counter 340. Out of one U and into a different U. Since the U-shaped areas are not that wide, all the lines for the various counters snake together at the entrance of the U, so it is difficult to see where the lines separate. Our line for counter 340 ended up at Scandinavian Airlines. Since we were heading to Dublin on Aer Lingus, I suspected something might be amiss.

Back out to the big screen. We were now checking in at counter 370, in a different U. By the time we figured out which line was ours, we ended up last in line. As the Aer Lingus clerk scanned our passports, no alarms went off. First hurdle crossed. Next came Passport Control. I went right with my EU Passport, and Kathy went left with her U.S. Passport. No alarms went off, so we crossed hurdle two successfully. No alarms again at Passport Control in Ireland. We were home free, for the time being.

— § —

The Celtic Tiger has resurfaced. According to the taxi driver who took us from the airport to our Airbnb in Charlotte Quay Dock, Ireland has the fastest growing economy in Europe. Although taxi drivers know everything, or at least have an opinion about everything, I had my doubts. Seeing all the construction cranes in and around downtown Dublin added credibility to his claim. When we went to our first restaurant in Dublin's technology district, the area in which our Airbnb was located, and paid 18 Euro for a hamburger, I was convinced. Fries were extra.

The introduction of the European Union in 1993 and the implementation of the Euro in 2002 have had a profound effect on Dublin. During our week stay, our taxi drivers included: Brendan Jeffries, Michael Feeney, P.J. Boyle, Anthony Phillips, Waqua Latif, Violet Doran, Nicholas Murphy, Balvinder Gaba, Femi Adebesin, Keith Barry, Zafar Hussain, David O'Shea, Karl O'Halloran, Amadu Bah, and Sunny Okagbue. One of the Irish sounding drivers was actually South African, so that puts the percentage of non-Irish drivers at 43 percent, which is low for folks we encountered throughout Dublin's service sector. Of the four folks who waited on us at Sweetman's Irish Pub, one of our favorites, none was Irish: Venezuela, Spain, Bulgaria, and Poland.

I don't know if every capital city has its own song, but Dublin does, and the song is *Molly Malone*. At least, it is the unofficial anthem of Dublin, so dedicated, along with Molly's statue, by the Lord Mayor of Dublin during the city's 1988 Millennium celebration. According to Wikipedia, while the first printed version of the song *Molly Malone* appeared in 1857, and then again in 1878, no one appears to be given credit for writing the song.

Everyone has heard the song *Molly Malone*, apparently everyone except Frank, which now leads me to question his smarts. If you don't remember the words, the first stanza goes:

> *In Dublin's fair city*
> *Where the girls are so pretty*
> *I first set my eyes on sweet Molly Malone*
> *As she wheeled her wheelbarrow*
> *Through streets broad and narrow*
> *Crying "cockles and mussels, alive, alive, oh"*
> *Alive, alive, oh*
> *Alive, alive, oh*
> *Crying "cockles and mussels, alive, alive, oh"*

Now I got to thinking that after 150 years, perhaps it was time to come up with a more modern version. So, I penned the following:

> *In Ireland's main city*
> *Where bartenders are pithy*
> *I first set my eyes on that creamy brown stout*
> *They filled their pint glasses*
> *And served thirsty masses*
> *Crying "here is your Guinness, now Slainté to you"*
> *Now Slainté to you*
> *Now Slainté to you*
> *Crying "here is your Guinness, now Slainté to you"*

Catchy, don't you think?

We visit Ireland on average about every five years, and every time we go there, I am reminded of Ireland's tragic history and the massive injustices the British Government and the British aristocracy heaped upon the Irish people over many centuries. I want to stay angry, but I don't and wonder why. Surely, there are enough sad Irish songs to remind me. Maybe it is "out of sight, out of mind." Maybe repression, although I did not personally experience injustice. Or maybe I am just too busy leading an Irish emigrant's life in my promised land. Regardless, these trips help me to "never forget," but in a constructive way.

On this visit, three events brought the message back in a most powerful way. The first was the trip to the EPIC Irish Emigration Museum, which is a reasonably new attraction in Dublin. The museum is housed in the lower level of a former customs warehouse on the north bank of the river Liffey. The exhibit, which takes about two hours to appreciate adequately, is a static display, augmented by computer generated, eye witness audiovisual stories. It guides you through room after room tracing Irish history, the Irish diaspora, the treacherous journeys the emigrants endured, the impact on Ireland's population, and the wealth of talent the destination countries received.

The second event was a guided tour of the Kilmainham Jail, an attraction I had overlooked on previous trips to Dublin. The jail opened in 1796 and closed in 1924, shortly after the end of the Irish civil war. Fourteen leaders of the 1916 Irish Easter Rising were executed here by British firing squads. What is perhaps more tragic is that the Irish Free State Provisional Government (required allegiance to the British Crown by treaty) executed more than 90 supporters of a true Irish Republic (no allegiance to Britain and return of the northern six counties to Ireland) during Ireland's brief civil war.

The third event involved taking a guided historical tour of Dublin conducted by a professor of history from Trinity College. This walking tour focused on the early Viking settlers who conquered what is now the area called Dublin, followed by the Norman invaders, and finally the British conquerors. The professor provided historical perspective on the famine and the resulting diaspora and on the Irish struggle for independence. We ended the tour in the courtyard of Dublin Castle, where on January 16, 1922, the Union Jack was lowered and the Irish flag was raised, ushering in the provisional government of the Irish Free State.

The words of the Trinity College professor and the displays in the EPIC Museum reintroduced me to the fact that the Irish potato famine (1845 to 1852) was not just an Irish event. The potato blight also affected potato crops in England and other European countries, with documentation showing that Belgium was affected as much as Ireland. What made the potato blight in Ireland a famine but not a famine in Belgium was based on the government's approach. Belgium stopped exporting food to other countries and instituted policies focused on feeding its own people.

The professor became emotional as he discussed that at this time in Ireland, the Irish people could not vote, could not hold office, could not own land, and, in certain cases, could not even own a horse. Historical records show that the British government viewed the Irish as a sub-human race. Communications between government officials, even newspaper articles, referred to the Irish as "monkeys." This potato blight in Ireland provided a convenient solution for reducing the population of Ireland, and all the British government and the British aristocracy in Ireland had to do was – nothing. Let nature take its course: problem solved.

As a result, the potato blight became a potato famine. Over 1 million died in Ireland of starvation or diseases associated with malnutrition. Over 1.5 million emigrated to Australia, New Zealand, Canada, the United States, South America, Europe, and Africa. Of those who boarded ships to take them to their promised land, approximately 40 percent died on their journey. To add insult to injury, according to our Kilmainham Jail tour guide, during this time, it became a crime to be a vagrant. Since there was no food and no work, thousands became vagrants and were thrown in Kilmainham Jail, the youngest of whom was five years old and convicted of stealing provisions. At least the vagrants got a modicum of food in jail.

The EPIC Emigration Museum does a great job of painting the positive effects of the Irish diaspora with the not so good side of that same period of Irish history. It does a superb job of documenting the contributions that the Irish have made to societies across the globe. In fact, 22 presidents of the United States have ancestors from Ireland. Equally important, we can't forget what Arthur Guinness and John Jameson did for Ireland; or perhaps *to* Ireland is more accurate.

— § —

Speaking of Arthur and John, I did my best to introduce our nephew Frank to both of them at every available opportunity. Since Frank had just turned 18 and that is the legal drinking age in Ireland, I felt it my patriotic duty to contribute to Frank's delinquency, strictly as a thank you for bringing our Apostille certified marriage certificates with him from Indianapolis.

In addition to the Emigration Museum, the Kilmainham Jail, and the historical walking tour, we did the hop-on, hop-off bus, walked St. Stephens Green, visited churches, visited Trinity College and marveled at the human technology used to create the Book of Kells in 800 A.D., visited Peterson's Pipe Store, walked Grafton Street twice, ate a full Irish breakfast at Lombard's pub, trekked through Temple Bar, drank Guinness and ate fish and chips in a few pubs while listening to live Irish music. And smoked cigars and drank Jameson.

While Dublin's restaurants are good, few we visited were memorable. Two are worth noting: SOLE, a high-end fish and steak restaurant in the city center, and Asador, also a fish and steak restaurant but a little removed from the city center. Both had excellent food, superb service, and delightful atmospheres. As luck would have it, there was an Italian coffee and pastry shop around the corner from our Airbnb, so I did not have to forego my morning cappuccino and croissant. All I needed to do next was order a seat belt extender from Amazon for our flight back to Italy.

On Tuesday, we saw Frank off to his flight back to Indianapolis, and we headed back to Rome with our Apostille documents in hand. No alarms went off as Kathy went through Passport Control in Rome's airport. We picked up Jack and headed back to Perugia home base to decompress, do laundry, and start a weight loss program. Maybe.

Chapter Eighteen

Verona – Pescara

Thursday, August 9 to Sunday, August 19

Kathy's grandfather on her mother's side, Antonio Ianniccari (1926-1986), and her great grandfather, Leonello Ianniccari (1879-1961), were born in Loreto Aprutino in the province of Pescara, which is about a three-hour drive from Perugia. After our Dublin trip, we were planning on recuperating for a week and then heading to Pescara for three days and see what we might find out about Kathy's relatives. Then I opened an email from Alis, Kathy's cousin's wife, and our recuperation plans went out the window.

If you were to look up "Energizer Bunny" in the dictionary, you might find Alis' picture next to the definition. Alis is a beautiful person and a brilliant attorney who gave up a promising career as a partner in a Delaware law firm to become general counsel for a precious metals company. Married to Kathy's cousin, Christopher, a physician, Alis and Chris have four boys ages 13 to five. The six of them, along with another family of five, were finishing up a vacation in Venice, after spending time in Spain and Croatia.

Seven of the travelling caravan of 11 were going back to the United States, but Alis and her three oldest boys were heading to Verona for a couple of days and wanted us to meet them there. Besides traveling all over the world for her job, Alis speaks Russian, finds time to be an amazing mom, is a gourmet cook, wine connoisseur, and avid reader – the kind of person you want to hate but can't. We could not pass up spending time with her and her three distinctly different but extremely talented and intelligent boys, so after two days' rest, we packed our bags again, loaded Jack in the car, and began a five-hour drive to Verona.

The main reason Alis and the boys were traveling to Verona was to see the Santuario Della Madonna Della Corona or the Sanctuary/Shrine of Our Lady of the Corona, which is built into the side of a mountain that lies about 45 minutes north and slightly west of Verona. "Corona" has several meanings, two of which appear to apply here. Per Wikipedia, one is a "rarefied, brilliant, and bright gaseous envelope surrounding the sun and other stars visible to the human eye under certain conditions." The other is "the overhanging part near the top of a classical cornice, having a flat outer surface."

According to popular legend, the story, which I have synopsized from the brochure I purchased, goes like this. On a warm June night in 1522, the villagers in the valley below Baldo Mountain saw a brilliant light hovering for some time slightly below the top of the mountain. Intrigued by the sight, the next day, several villagers hiked to the top of the mountain, but unable to see anything directly below, they devised a rope and basket system to lower one of the members to the area of interest. After some distance, the villager came upon a large flat shelf cut into the mountain, and resting there was a statue of the Virgin Mary sitting with the body of the dying Christ lying across her knees.

The villager retrieved the statue and brought it to the mountain top to the rest of the curious hikers, who marveled at the find but were unsure what to think, so they returned to the village and placed the statue in the village chapel. When they awoke the next morning, the statue was missing. Down in the basket one more time, and there the villager found the statue back on the horizontal shelf. The villager retrieved the statue, and the group of hikers returned it to the chapel a second time. The next morning the statue was missing again, and once again they found it on the horizontal shelf. This series of events was taken as a religious sign, and plans for the construction of a shrine to Our Lady of the Corona began.

As word of this incident spread, the villagers cut footpaths to the mountainside corona so more and more pilgrims could access the location. Eventually, several Knights of St. Giovanni Gerosolimitan from the island of Rhodes in Greece came on a pilgrimage and recognized the statue as one that disappeared from their island, where, according to legend, the statue was carried away by angels in June of 1522. That is one theory, but there are counter theories as to the exact dates of the existence of the statue and the evolution of the devotion surrounding its significance.

Regardless, enough people subscribed to one or another of these theories that construction began in 1625 on a more formal shrine. Various expansions and revisions took place over 400 years, with the current version of the sanctuary being completed between 1975 and 1978. While the sanctuary and the manner in which it is built into the mountain is stunning, its location on this flat 75-yard-wide precipice two thirds up the side of a sheer cliff is beyond description. From the main parking area, you can access the sanctuary via many hundred steps down, or you can traverse a long descending serpentine road, along which are built life-sized replicas of the stations of the cross. Religious significance aside, these bronze castings are impressive works of art in their own right.

Verona turned out to be our favorite non-mountaintop city in Italy. The city is reasonably level, so it is easy to navigate. It has an intriguing history. The Roman arena, an active concert and opera venue, is spectacular. The city's architecture is majestic. A beautiful river courses around and through the city. The shopping is on par with any other Italian city, and the restaurants are plentiful and excellent.

We were fortunate, with a little help from some locals, to stumble upon three amazing dining venues: Ristorante Maffei hidden just off Piazza Erbe, Ristorante Il Cenacolo just west behind Piazza Bra, and on our way back from the Shrine, the restaurant at Hotel Villa Cariola. At each place, we opted for the local Valpolicella della Casa, and were never disappointed. It is worth noting that after lunch at Ristorante Maffei, the waiter invited us to tour their exquisite wine cellar, which lies on the second and third level below the restaurant and just above some amazing Roman ruins, visible through glass floors, which they discovered while excavating for their wine cellar. Even Jack was invited on the tour.

Verona has several churches, and we visited two of them. The interior of the Church of St. Anastasia, Verona's largest church, with all its Veronese marble columns and granite carvings is absolutely spectacular, as good as any we have seen. Construction of the church, which was designed by two Dominican friars, began in 1290 A.D. and lasted on and off for 400 years. The Duomo, simply called the Cathedral Complex because it incorporates several buildings, although perhaps not as ornate, is remarkable in its own way.

— § —

We bid Alis and her boys, all of whom took turns spoiling the heck out of Jack, farewell for their flight home from Venice, and we headed back to Perugia for a day's rest before traveling to Pescara. Pescara is both a city as well as a province on the Adriatic Sea in the region of Abruzzo. Italy has 20 regions, and within these regions lie 107 provinces. Umbria is a region with only two provinces: Perugia and Terni. The region with the largest number of provinces is Lombardia, with 12.

Our day of rest, Wednesday, was also an Italian holiday, the Feast of the Assumption of the Blessed Mary. The next day we headed out for Pescara, with a stop first in Loreto Aprutino to do some ancestry research. Our route took us south past Assisi and Spello to the town of Foligno. From there we drove east to the town of Porto Sant'Elpidio on the Adriatic Sea, and south along the coast, then slightly inland to Loreto Aprutino. The drive was extremely beautiful, or at least the part that we saw. From Foligno to Sant'Elpidio we passed through 35 tunnels. From Sant'Elpidio to Pescara, we transited another 20 tunnels.

That afternoon, we arrived in Loreto Aprutino, which turned out to be a small but charming hilltop town of 7,369 people, and drove directly to the Comune di Loreto (city government office). Closed. The Police Station. Closed. The Office of Immigration. Closed. After the fact, we learned that in August, one day holidays, in this case also the holiday of Ferragosto, sometimes become two-day or perhaps three-day holidays. In a town of 7,400 folks, you probably don't get a lot of opposition to really long weekends.

So, what to do? We were stopped at an intersection in the center of town contemplating our next move, when I looked to the left at the town's main piazza and saw of group of 12 men, ages 60 to 80, sitting on park benches and chatting either about the weather, the world's problems, or about their wives. And why not? It was a holiday. We parked the car close to the group, and then with our ancestry PowerPoint slides in hand, I walked into the lion's den, and asked if the name "Ianniccari" rang any bells with anyone in the group.

Finally, the group had a real-world problem it might be able to solve. They all started talking at once. The most vocal and animated was the youngest, who was clearly under the influence of alcohol. The group quickly admonished him, and he returned to his seat on the bench, not to be heard from again. After much discussion, one of the group pulled out his phone and called someone named Lorenzo. The man with the phone signaled us to wait, and all in the group nodded approval of their consensus decision making. If anyone in town knew the name "Ianniccari" it would be Lorenzo. After all, he was the city's retired mail carrier.

Lorenzo arrived about 10 minutes later and after introductions, no English so far, signaled us to follow him. With Jack in tow, we headed deeper into the town, not sure where we were going or what we were going to accomplish when we got there. After three blocks, Lorenzo stopped and yelled up to a window on the third floor of one of the buildings, and seconds later a gentleman stuck his head out the window and signaled to Lorenzo. Five minutes later, the gentleman emerged and introduced himself. His name was Noel McCarthy, apparently one of the town's few English-speaking residents. We learned that Noel happened to be from Dublin, Ireland, and was married to a woman from Mullingar, the town I lived in before we emigrated to the U.S.

The four of us and Jack headed off still deeper into town and soon arrived at Lorenzo's home. Inside the door to the right was the kitchen/dining/living room.

Straight ahead was a stairway to the upper levels, and to the left was a small rest room. Inside the kitchen was a table that sat eight – a table almost as large as the room itself. Trying to be sensitive, I explained that I would stay outside with Jack, and let Noel do all the interpreting and fact finding. Lorenzo would not take no for an answer, so inside we went.

Jack and I stopped at the kitchen entrance, for there was little space inside the room itself. Lorenzo and his wife were there, either Lorenzo's or his wife's parents were there, five other women were inside, either friends or relatives of Lorenzo's family, and Kathy and Noel. With great deliberation, they passed around the PowerPoint sheet with names and birth and marriage dates, and each person, in turn, failed to recognize anyone by the name Ianniccari. They agreed that Marissa might know since she worked at the Office of Vital Statistics, and that should we decide to return tomorrow, Noel would show us where Marissa's office was located.

The grandfather did not want to miss out on the action, so the five of us and Jack walked back to the main piazza where Noel pointed out our destination for tomorrow. As a thank you, I offered to buy a round of adult beverages, so we secured a table in one of the two small restaurants on the piazza and continued to discuss our ancestry search. During this time, Noel suggested exchanging email addresses, and he said that he would inquire with Marissa about any relatives still living in Loreto Aprutino and notify us if a return trip was in order. Good plan.

— § —

We departed Loreto Aprutino and about 30 minutes later, we arrived at the Carlton Hotel on the beach promenade of Pescara. The promenade is easily four miles long with a separate asphalt bike path and 20-yard-wide pedestrian sidewalk lined with natural stone. The promenade was impressive and beautiful. There is not a lot of wave action on the western shore of the Adriatic Sea, so maintaining a pristine beach appears to be uncomplicated.

The beach is close to 200 yards deep, and most of the beach access is private, controlled by a plethora of private clubs. Each club has its own distinctive array of large stationary beach umbrellas set up in precise perpendicular lines to the shore. It is quite a sight to look for a mile in either direction and see thousands of multi-colored umbrellas dotting the beach.

That evening we dined at Ristorante Bluefin, a small but amazing seafood-only restaurant two blocks from our hotel. We both had the grilled octopus appetizer. I had the grilled Amberjack steak which was an inch thick and seasoned and cooked to perfection, and Kathy had the lightly breaded and flash fried seafood dinner.

The next evening after our trip to Chieti, we dined at Regina Elena where the service was as good as we have ever experienced. We each had a different pasta with seafood as our "primi," and then opted for the whole Branzino baked in a salt shell. Without a doubt, this was the most delicious fish dish we have ever eaten.

Our trip to Chieti, another case where the province and the town have the same name, was made on behalf of Kathy's cousin George, whose grandfather was from Chieti. George knew his grandfather's and grandmother's names and that they emigrated to the U.S. around 1900. With just that information to go on, we headed for the city government office in Chieti, which happened to be open. At a population of more than 50,000, Chieti is a very large hilltop city, so finding a retired mail carrier and a guy from Dublin to help us was probably not in the cards.

No one inside the lobby of the government office was able to understand me, even with my handy iPhone translation app. All I wanted to know was what steps would be involved in getting birth and marriage records for someone born "around" 1875 and married shortly "before" 1900. Three different greeters referred me to one of the six lobby windows containing a sign for birth and marriage records. The lady behind the bullet proof glass had no clue as to what I was trying to accomplish.

Undaunted, we just hung around the lobby of the government office, much to Jack's chagrin, and asked everyone who arrived if he or she spoke English. After an hour, I found a pregnant woman whose English was wonderful, and who agreed to assist. She explained to the lady behind the bullet proof glass what I needed.

As it turned out, this office had records only from 1903 and newer, but she did provide a slip of paper with instructions on how to search Chieti's archive database. Back at our hotel, I was able to find George's grandfather's marriage and birth records, an achievement that made George's day.

We spent Saturday wandering the promenade of Pescara and just being lazy. That evening we dined at Chef Nestor's Sushi Ristorante, which was as good as any we have ever frequented. In the meantime, our new friend from Loreto Aprutino, Noel McCarthy, had been busy on our behalf, and his efforts started to produce some substantial results.

While we were in Chieti trying to find an English-speaking person at the Comune di Chieti, I received a text from Noel McCarthy. He told me that he posted a message to several message boards requesting that he be contacted by anyone with information on anyone by the name of Ianniccari from Loreto Aprutino. Noel was hopeful that his efforts would produce something of value on Kathy's ancestors.

While Noel was hopeful, Kathy and I were not quite that enthusiastic, especially since the retired mailman in a town of 7,400 people did not recognize the name Ianniccari among any of his former clients. But then again, had we not just stumbled into this same town of 7,400 people in the province of Pescara, and through a series of serendipitous events, run into a guy from Dublin who was married to a lady from the town in which I grew up? What are the odds of that? A good omen, perhaps?

Apparently so. On Saturday night while we were still in Pescara, I received an email from Noel saying that he had heard from a resource in Milan who had information on the family Ianniccari, and that this person would be contacting Noel and us shortly. What comes next is hard to believe.

The gentleman in Milan was Maurizio Casalena, and his hobby is doing ancestry trees. Maurizio's relatives also happen to be from the town of Loreto Aprutino, and he had recently been focusing all his ancestry efforts documenting families from Loreto Aprutino. Sunday morning, before we checked out of our hotel, I received two emails from Maurizio to which he attached two Adobe Acrobat files and an ancestry diagram.

As I started to review the files Maurizio sent me, my sense of disbelief grew at a geometrical rate. Maurizio had already traced the Ianniccari family from Giuliano Ianniccari born in 1725, to Zopito (1751) to Pasquale (1798) to Cesidio (1831) to Leonello (1879), which was where Kathy's efforts ran into a road block, to Antonio (1906) to Kathy's mom, Linda (1931) to Kathy who is married to Daniel D. Houlihan!

There I was, sitting on a Sunday morning at my laptop in a hotel in Pescara looking at the Ianniccari family tree that starts in 1725 and ends with my name, done by a person in Milan, not related to or having any knowledge of any person inside the family tree.

I was astonished. What are the odds of coming to a small Italian town on Thursday, a day when all the government offices are supposed to be open but are closed, taking a chance that one of 12 men sitting in the town square might recognize a family name, that one of the men would be the brother of a retired mail carrier, whose call to his brother would lead us to a guy from Dublin, who on his own initiative posts to a message board which is read by a guy in Milan, who already happens to have the complete ancestry tree of the family in question, who then emails the tree to me, all in essentially a span of three days?

Now all five children of Linda (Ianniccari) Nelson have one side of their mother's family tree in their possession. In a couple of days, Kathy's sister, Christine, and husband Dave would be here for more than a week, so there were certain to be ancestry discussions, adventures, and tons of giggles in our immediate future.

CHAPTER NINETEEN

THE LADIES OF POLIZIA NAZIONALE

MONDAY, AUGUST 20 TO MONDAY, AUGUST 27

I trust you remember the unfriendly, face-making, head-shaking clerk behind Window 2 at the Polizia Nazionale? She was the one with whom Kathy and I first met and presented what we thought were all the completed and appropriate papers for Kathy's residency card. She and her English-speaking supervisor set us straight on what was "required" – as opposed to what we were led to believe was needed.

A couple of weeks later, you recall, Giuseppe and I had the marathon session with both of them, including Katherina from the Information Office, at the end of which they reluctantly agreed to start Kathy's residency card application so our trip to Ireland and back to Italy would not be compromised due to lack of appropriate documentation.

While in Ireland, we picked up the two copies of our Apostille certified marriage record from Kathy's nephew Frank. Once back in Perugia, I returned with Giuseppe to the ladies of the Polizia Nazionale to make sure that our Apostille document met with their approval before we hired a translator and made another trip to the Justice Department to have them officially stamped.

Sometimes, unexpected wide swings in human behavior are really hard to explain. On this visit, we first met with the English-speaking supervisor and refreshed her memory on our case, which didn't take too much refreshing at all. The Apostille document appeared to meet with her approval. Then she and Giuseppe approached Window 2, to the dismay and disapproval of the five folks already waiting in line at Window 2, where our favorite clerk, after reviewing the document, nodded her approval – even with a big smile and a wave to me.

When the English-speaking supervisor reiterated the need to get the document translated and stamped by the Justice Department, Giuseppe went into what I can only describe as smooth-talking overdrive. When he finished explaining all the trials, tribulations, and money we had been through to get to this point, the supervisor agreed to save us more bureaucratic agony, and stated she would do the translation herself and stamp the Polizia Nazionale seal of approval on the document.

This unprecedented and completely out of character move even surprised the Window 2 clerk, but she, after a little hesitation, nodded approval. Before we left, both ladies independently wanted to know how Jack Daniels was doing. It appeared that Giuseppe and Jack Daniels had been quite an effective team at softening the hearts and minds of these ladies. I should have brought Jack with me on all our previous trips.

So where did this leave us regarding Kathy's residency card? Based on our latest visit, it looked like the Polizia Nazionale now had all the documents it needed. However, it couldn't go forward with Kathy's residency card until *my* residency was confirmed. But the law says that after 45 days, if a residency application has not been acted upon, then it is automatically approved.

As best I could determine, based on when my application was officially submitted and the 45-day rule, I would be an official resident of Perugia around September 8. However, the process of approving Kathy's residency card would take two to four months after that, so the likelihood of her having the card before we left to return home to the U.S. was doubtful. Since there was nothing more to do on our end other than wait for my official residency approval, the quest for Kathy's residency card was on hold until then. At least Kathy's unfettered exit from the EU in November appeared assured.

Mountains – Monasteries – Monks – and Beer. It has such a nice ring to it, and for me conjures up images of a scenic yet serene life dedicated to holiness and hops. While Italy is about wine and pasta and hilltop towns, it would seem that a trip to see beer brewing monks in the mountains would be a worthwhile side adventure. And so it was that a month before Kathy's sister, Chris, and husband Dave, arrived, Dave sent me an email asking me to check out the Benedictine Monks of Norcia and see if a visit there was realistic. Having never heard of the monks, as was the case with Dave, I was excited to see what I could find.

As it turns out, Norcia is at the base of the Sibillini Mountains National Park and is a delightful one hour and 20-minute drive from Villa Nuba. The Monastery of Saint Benedict in Monte is situated above the ancient town of Norcia, or "Nursia" as it was called in Latin, the birthplace of St. Benedict, who is credited with founding European monasticism. The beer the monks brew is called "Birra Nursia," and the monks have a pretty slick and sophisticated website to market their products, one which appears to belie their vow of poverty. I imagine the website was built with donations from beer lovers all over the world.

After receiving Dave's message, the name Norcia sounded awfully familiar, but I could not remember why until we started paying attention to restaurant menus. Per Wikipedia, Norcia is known as the pork capital of Italy and is hailed for its skilled butchers (norcinos) and the charcuterie and salumi they produce. Well over a thousand years ago, the norcinos were so skilled, they were often asked to work on humans in the absence of medical professionals. While today we use the term "quack" to describe an incompetent medical doctor, by the 1500s Italians started using the term "norcino" in the same fashion.

The Sibillini mountains, part of the Apennine mountain chain, and the valley in which Norcia sits has an abundance of oak trees. The acorns from the oak trees were consumed by the pigs and wild boar in the area, which helped produce delicious meats from both animals, which generated the need for great butchers to dissect the animals and preserve their meats for shipment and sale – all of which, over the centuries, led to the town gaining the reputation of producing the best pork and having the best butchers in Italy. But Norcia is also known for black truffles, lentils, and cheeses, especially pecorino, which you will see, in addition to pork, on restaurant menus throughout Umbria.

Back to the monks. The monks celebrate mass every day at 10:00 a.m. and during mass, among many other times during the day, they chant what is called the Sacred Office in Latin, sometimes known as Gregorian Chants. The key factor in our decision on which day to visit the monks was solved by the fact that they sell their beer only between 9:00 a.m. and noon on Saturday. Our plan, therefore, was to be in Norcia at 9:30 a.m., attend the 10:00 mass, taste and buy beer, have lunch, and then head to Orvieto for the afternoon.

In October of 2016, Norcia was near the epicenter of an earthquake that affected a large portion of Umbria. All of the churches in the town of Norcia were destroyed, including the large Basilica of Saint Benedict. The small church up on the hillside home of the monks sustained significant damage, but while it remained the only "standing" church in Norcia, it did suffer enough damage to make it uninhabitable. Government grants and beer sales are helping the monks restore their church and return to their former life. In the meantime, they have constructed a new modern wooden building to house their temporary church, living quarters and beer brewing operations.

The earthquake, the results of which are still painfully visible throughout the town, must have destroyed all signs to the abbey of the Benedictine monks, because even though we arrived in Norcia on schedule, we had a tough time finding any signs leading to the abbey. Neither Giselle nor our iPhone Google app nor passers-by were much help, mainly because the passers-by spoke only Italian. We did know that the abbey was near the Agriturismo Il Casale Degli Amici on the outskirts of town, which we eventually found, and we made it to the temporary abbey shortly after mass started.

We all entered the makeshift church and took our seats, Jack included. And why not? The website showed one of the monks with a dog. After getting seated, we realized that this was no ordinary mass because there was a gentleman without a beard officiating the mass, while everyone else around the altar had beards and shaved heads. We learned that two new monks were being sworn in to the order of the Benedictines, and the Cardinal was the guest officiant. What would have been a 45-minute mass was on the way to becoming a 90-minute service.

To the left of the altar were two rows of benches on which sat four monks, one of whom apparently noticed Jack, stood up and exited behind the altar. Within minutes, the rear door opened, and the monk motioned Jack and me to the exit. Unlike the three toddlers wandering around the small church and making a ton of noise, Jack was being perfectly quiet; regardless, we complied with the monk's request. Once outside, the monk advised us that dogs were not allowed in church, to which I replied that St. Francis would probably have allowed Jack in his church. The monk smiled but stuck to his guns.

I had a lovely conversation with this monk, whose English was perfect — because he was from Arizona. I learned that he and three other monks were priests and the other eight in the community were brothers, several of whom were from the United States. Before he returned to the service, I asked the priest if he could recommend a good restaurant for lunch. Without hesitation, he recommended the Agriturismo Degli Amici and offered to make a reservation for us, a gesture I gladly accepted.

After the service, we headed down the hill about 200 yards from the abbey to an open field where a temporary gravel road led to a 25-foot trailer, which served as the temporary beer sales office. With no opportunity to taste the monks' brew, Dave and I purchased a few bottles of their blonde beer and their dark beer, and then left for lunch at the Agriturismo about a half a mile away. Lunch, which turned out to be excellent, was an offering of pasta and meat dishes made from all things Norcia.

— § —

Chris and Dave were visiting for only four days before we all headed to Venice for three days. On Friday, we spent the morning touring Perugia and the afternoon in Spello. Saturday was Norcia followed by Orvieto for the afternoon, which turned out to be quite a favorite city once we had gotten to see more of it. Sunday, we spent in Montepulciano, and Monday we spent the day in Assisi.

One final note on Norcia. When Dave called his daughter who lives in Houston, and told her, among other things, about our trip to the Monks of Norcia, she replied, "Wow, what a coincidence, I happen to have their CD in my car and listen to the monks all the time." This is a small world after all.

Kathy's cousin George, a descendant of the Rossi clan from Chieti, and his wife, Lorraine, were supposed to accompany Chris and Dave to Italy. Lorraine recently suffered a serious knee injury doing a summersault off a bar stool, and they had to cancel their trip, a significant setback since neither one had ever been to Italy.

Prior travel arrangements tending to be non-refundable, Chris and Dave journeyed to Venice by train on previously purchased tickets, while Kathy and I drove to Venice sans George and Lorraine.

While Chris and Dave went to their delightful Airbnb right on the grand canal in Venice, Kathy and I took a water taxi to the Hilton Molino Stucky on the island of Giudecca, which sits on the main water highway across from Venice. Without a doubt, the Molino Stucky is the most exquisite Hilton property we have visited.

The hotel is a series of four buildings erected in the early to mid 1800s by Giovanni(y) Stucky. For over 100 years, the buildings housed a flour mill and later on a bread and pasta making factory. However, by 1955 technology and competition and cost factors caused both factories to shutter their doors.

The property stood vacant for nearly 50 years until Hilton took it over and created its waterfront masterpiece. The imagination and engineering involved in creating this property is hard to comprehend. Throughout the hotel are storyboards with before and after pictures documenting the hotel's history and attesting to the extent of disrepair that existed before the restoration, and to the imagination it took to seamlessly insert hotel, dining, shopping, spa, and conference facilities inside the shell of a former factory.

Chris and Dave had visited Venice with their son Frank only nine months before, so Dave was willing to be our official tour guide for this part of our adventure. While water taxis are expensive but get you directly from point A to point B in the shortest amount of time, the Venice water buses, called vaporettos, are significantly less expensive but require patience and plenty of time.

Under Dave's tutelage, we purchased a three-day vaporetto pass for 40 Euro per person. These passes not only allowed us to go anywhere in Venice during our three days but also to go to the island of Murano, the home of Italian glass, about a 30-minute ride, and to Burano, the home of Italian lace, an additional 30-minute ride from Murano.

Having always thought of Venice as an island, I never felt the urge to investigate further until this trip. Per Wikipedia, what we know as Venice is actually made up of 118 separate islands connected by foot bridges and narrow waterways. And the foundations for the buildings on these islands is — wood! Wood pilings were driven side by side down into the mud and sandy soil of the many lagoon islands that existed below what is now Venice. Since the area around Venice had limited forests, most of the wood pilings came from trees grown in Croatia, Slovenia, and Montenegro.

Apparently, wood needs oxygen and microorganisms to decay, but since these pilings are submerged in seawater and mud, over time the mineral rich seawater and lack of oxygen cause the wood to petrify and harden into concrete-like pilings. Once the pile driving was completed, the pilings were cut off slightly above water level, then timbers were laid across the pilings which became the foundation for the wooden or stone homes built above. Millions upon millions upon millions of pilings were eventually used in construction of the foundations of each of the islands that make up Venice.

Venice has 32 churches and 23 museums. We did not visit any museums and entered only four churches: Santa Redentore, San Gorgio Maggiore, Santa Maria Gloriosa Dei Frari, and Santo Giovanni e Paolo. True to form, the first two churches were glorious on the outside, and ordinary, for an Italian church that is, on the inside. The last two churches were quite plain on the outside but were loaded with magnificent art work, stone sculptures, and wood carvings on the inside.

Our dining adventures in Venice were very good, but two particular restaurants stood out as excellent: Osteria Ai Artisti and Trattoria Antiche Carampane. On the Giudecca side, Osteria Ae Botti was also excellent. Venice is hard not to love; however, it becomes a lot harder to love when there are a hundred thousand tourists clogging every part of the city and maxing out the capacity of every vaporetto. Were we to go back, I would avoid June through September. Dave and Chris vacationed in Venice in December and found it a delightful time to explore the city.

While age, tourism, and weather have taken a toll on the buildings in Venice, the Adriatic Sea is posing an even greater threat to the city. News articles warn that the slightly rising level of the Adriatic is a significant concern, especially during heavy storms when a few extra inches of rising tide, which is normally minimal, could have a devastating effect. The best engineering minds in the world have been challenged to provide a solution to this perplexing issue. So, if you have never been to Venice and are planning on visiting at some point, going sooner may be better than later.

— § —

Our next adventure with Chris and Dave, and one orchestrated by them, brought us from Venice to the town of Marostica, not too far from the city of Vicenza, where every two years a live chess match is played and the match acts as the centerpiece of a colorful medieval festival. This extravaganza involves approximately 600 of Marostica's inhabitants.

For two and a half hours we witnessed: royal dignitaries of every rank, shape, size, and age dressed in authentic medieval garb; town criers, court jesters, and minstrels; religious dignitaries; buglers and drummers; flag bearers and precision flag throwers; knights and their mounts; friars and their asses; archers and flaming arrows; fire rings and fireworks; all choreographed in a well told story, much like a Broadway play but performed on a far grander scale.

According to the brochure that accompanied our tickets, in 1454 Lord Taddeo Parisio had two daughters, the oldest and apparently most beautiful, Lionora, and the youngest and less beautiful, Oldrada. At that time, two well-to-do gentlemen were vying for the hand of Lionora. Rather than have a sword fight to determine the winner of Lionora's hand, as was the custom, Lord Parisio dictated that the two suitors would play a chess match, and that the winner would have the hand of Lionora in marriage, and the loser, the hand of Oldrada.

Of such stories, festivals are born, and the idea for this particular festival was born shortly after the end of World War II by the town's chess players. To serve as the stage for their play, they built a human size chess board in the middle of the town piazza. Since the original chess moves were not recorded, the play mimics famous historical chess matches, with a different match being played during each of the four biennial performances. Thanks to Dave, we had seats on the top row at about the 40-yard line to witness the pomp and circumstance of this colorful and exciting medieval extravaganza.

— § —

We bid Chris and Dave farewell as they headed to Vicenza and then Rome and then home, while we motored to Milan to meet with Maurizio Casalena, the gentleman who read the message posted by Noel McCarthy from Loreto Aprutino and the next day emailed me the complete Ianniccari family tree. Maurizio advised us that if we were ever in Milan, he would be thrilled to give us a tour of his beautiful city. While Milan was not part of our Italy plan, we could not pass up the opportunity to have a personal local guide.

Kathy and I arrived at the Hilton Milan and met Maurizio who took us on a four-hour, 16,000 step walking tour of Milan, a trip, in retrospect, we are so glad we decided to undertake. Maurizio was a superb guide whose love of Milan was readily apparent at every stop we made. The walk from our hotel to the center of Milan, a distance of close to two miles, was a lot like walking through the newer parts of Munich.

More than one third of the buildings in Milan were destroyed during the bombing campaigns of World War II, so the outer city has a modern feel about it. But once you reach the city center, Milan takes on that old world feel and a spectacular scene unfolds: the Duomo, the Piazza Del Duomo, the Galleria Vittorio Emanuele II, La Scala Opera House, and so much more.

So, which Milan attraction had the longest line? Not the Duomo, Milan's Italian Gothic Cathedral which took 600 years to build, and is the third largest in the world with hundreds of spires and more than 3,000 statues on its exterior alone. No indeed; the longest line was at Starbucks. According to Maurizio, Italy had been one of a few countries in the world without a Starbucks. The first Starbucks in Italy opened in Milan the day before we arrived, and as we passed the coffee shop around 3:00 p.m., the line to get in was two blocks long.

We skipped Starbucks and continued our tour. We had hoped to see Da Vinci's Last Supper, but viewing appointments were being taken for the month of December. That evening we had a wonderful dinner with Maurizio, his wife Monica, and their daughter, Francesca, at Ristorante Santa Virginia in the Brera area of Milan. All three speak beautiful English, so the conversation and wine flowed freely.

The four-and-a-half-hour trip back to Perugia went smoothly, and we picked up Jack from his pensione the following morning. Jack's skin still looked nice and clean. Shortly after we got home, Jack ate half a bar of Dove soap, so now his intestines would be the same. We awaited the fallout from his mischievous act.

Chapter Twenty-One

Residency — Maurizio — Norcia — Montalcino — Gubbio

Tuesday, September 9 to Saturday, October 6

After a few days of keen observation, Jack's soap opera produced little drama. No Emmy was awarded and, thankfully, no enema needed. Over the next few days, we decompressed, did laundry, and ran some errands. With nothing firm planned for a few weeks after returning from our Venice, Marostica, and Milan adventures, I took advantage of the down time to inquire into the status of my Perugia residency.

My application for residency was supposed to have been approved around September 8. Curious as to whether that had actually happened, on September 17, a week after our return, I headed to the Comune di Perugia office I visited last time, one within walking distance from Villa Nuba, to see if the office could provide a status.

Two ladies in this administrative office spoke English, so explaining why I was in their office was easy enough; in addition, I had all my papers with me as backup. I expected them to hand me my approval dated the day after the 45 days expired. No such luck.

They were willing, however, to type up the approval while I was there. Any chance they would send it to the Polizia Nazionale? No, I would have to take care of that myself. All I needed to do at this point was go to the closest tobacco store and purchase another 16 Euro tax stamp. With stamp in hand I returned to the office, and within 10 minutes, I walked out of the Comune building as an official resident of Perugia, effective September 17, 2018.

With Giuseppe out of town again, the next afternoon we headed to the Polizia Nazionale on our own to give my "approved" residency application to the face making, head shaking clerk at Window 2, or to the scraggly-haired English-speaking supervisor. Neither person was available, no other English speakers were available, and the lines at the windows were jammed. The next day, we returned late morning and encountered the same situation. On Thursday, I returned by myself and got there when the office opened and found the English-speaking supervisor.

She worked with a different clerk to ensure that my formal residency approval was added to Kathy's residency card application. We had now overcome all the obstacles that Perugia's bureaucracy had thrown in our way. With no expectation of ever seeing Kathy's residency card before we departed, I left the Polizia Nazionale for the last time. Unless, of course, I was returned there in handcuffs for driving without a license.

— § —

There are some very nice people in this world who get great pleasure out of doing things for others and expect nothing in return. Maurizio Casalena happens to be one of them. As you recall, Maurizio's family was from Loreto Aprutino, the same town as Kathy's grandfather (her mother's dad), so Maurizio had previously constructed family trees on most residents of Loreto Aprutino.

While the Ianniccari family history that Maurizio provided was truly amazing, we had previously determined that Kathy could not pursue dual citizenship with Italy through that branch of her family. The issue had to do with her grandfather, born in Italy, getting naturalized in the U.S. before Kathy's mother was born, thereby breaking the bloodline.

While in Milan, we treated Maurizio and his family to dinner as a thank you for all he had done for Kathy and her siblings on the Ianniccari family tree. Apparently, our simple gesture of thanks, unbeknownst to us, compelled Maurizio to put forth a similar effort to construct Kathy's ancestry on the Zeccola branch of her Italian family tree.

Our research on the Zeccola side of Kathy's ancestry appeared to provide a more reliable path to dual citizenship since the naturalization aspect did not appear to be a stumbling block, a fact we would still have to verify. The bigger issue involved the fact that the Chicago research firm we had contracted with could not locate birth or marriage records on Kathy's great grandparents, Giuseppe and Maria Zeccola. Along came Maurizio to the rescue.

The ancestry research we had done before leaving the U.S. led us to believe that Giuseppe Zeccola was born in 1885 in Calabritto, province of Avellino, in the region of Campania. In the Ianniccari family tree Maurizio previously produced, there was a link to Catherine Zeccola who married Antonio Ianniccari (Kathy's grandfather), and through that link, Maurizio was able to find that Kathy's great grandfather and great grandmother were actually born in Muro Lucano, province of Potenza, in the region of Basilicata, in 1887 and 1889, respectively.

So, within a week of returning from Milan, we got an unexpected but deeply appreciated email from Maurizio, titled "Great News," which detailed his findings. We were blown away once again by his efforts on our behalf. In addition, Maurizio had called the Comune di Muro Lucano and determined that they not only had the birth records of Giuseppe and Maria and but also their marriage record.

Sometimes, timing is everything. As it turned out, we had previously planned on spending four days in Rome in October, followed by five days in Sorrento, with a day in between to allow us to stop in Calabritto and see what we might be able to find on Kathy's grandparents. Now all we had to do was drive from Rome to Muro Lucano, a little over two hours east of Naples and Sorrento, and pick up the three records. No need to go to Calabritto.

Not only that, Maurizio emailed us the authorization form we would need to pick up the Muro Lucano records, and set up an appointment time for us to do so. In addition, since he knew we would need Apostille certification for these records, he located the appropriate government certification office in Potenza, an hour drive from Muro Lucano in the same general direction as Sorrento. He also made an appointment for us at that office. A few days later, Maurizio provided a full ancestral tree and narrative on the Zeccola family from Muro Lucano. How in the world do you adequately thank a person like that?

— § —

With our bureaucratic battles behind us, our minds at ease, and our schedule for the month of October already well planned, we had some free time to continue exploring the area around Perugia before heading off to Rome and points south. We were so touched by our visit to the monks of Norcia and the earthquake aftermath we witnessed there that we decided to take a day and return to the town of Norcia, which we had not been able to see on our first visit.

Norcia is a small walled town, so it does not take a lot of effort to see most of its attractions. The Basilica of St. Benedict, which was a very large basilica, is still in shambles. The roof collapsed as did the right side and most of the left side. The front facade and a sizable portion of the rear are still standing but supported by scaffolding. I asked a police officer if they were rebuilding or going to tear down and replace with a new structure. As best he knew, the plan was to tear down and replace.

Many of the buildings have lengthy cracks that have since been repaired. Parts of the town's outer wall collapsed from the earthquake and remain in that state, and a few buildings are closed or condemned due to extensive damage. It is such a shame to see a quaint town like Norcia in such a sad state of affairs. But the people are gregarious and optimistic, the shops are busy, the restaurants are reasonably crowded, and the town continues to produce amazing meats and cheeses.

We headed to Norcia with three restaurant recommendations. One was a little outside the walled town, so we skipped it, a second was open only for dinner, and the third was closed for renovation. After checking with some locals, we ended up at Trattoria Locanda Del Teatro in the town's main square – directly across from the theater.

We started with a platter of Norcia meats and cheeses and the "vino rosso della casa." As you might suspect, the meats and cheeses were superb. We followed with homemade tagliatelle with wild boar sauce, a specialty of Norcia. It was the best wild boar sauce I had tasted since coming to Italy. The wine, an Umbrian Sangiovese, was delightful and cheap – 3 Euro a glass.

We enjoyed the wine so much that I investigated where I might be able to purchase it. I took a picture of the bottle and tracked down places that sold it. As it turns out, the wine is produced by a consortium of grape growers very near Assisi, who individually don't have enough grapes to produce their own wine, but as a consortium have tons of grapes and are able to produce gallons of wine.

I made my way to the Cantina Bettona Vetunna Wine Cooperative a few days after our Norcia visit. I went all out and bought six bottles of the wine we liked for 2.55 Euro each and six bottles of a Merlot/Sangiovese blend for 4 Euro each. A total of 39.30 Euro for the case. Both wines were very drinkable. But, if you are on a tight budget, you can bring your own five-gallon plastic container, and go to the petrol-looking metered wine pump and get as much wine as you need at a further discount. I only wish I had discovered this place the first week we arrived in Perugia.

Our next day trip was back to Montalcino, one of our favorite hilltop towns. When we were in Italy in 2015, our guide for Montalcino took us to a couple of wineries near the town in the morning. Then after touring the town itself, we

140

stopped for lunch at a tiny restaurant down a side street not too distant from the fortress. We enjoyed the restaurant so much in 2015 that I was determined to find it so we could visit it on this trip. Armed with only the pictures of the meal we enjoyed in 2015, I spent a few days of Internet research and found the restaurant – "Re Di Macchia."

After reacquainting ourselves with Montalcino, we headed to Re Di Macchia for lunch and were not disappointed. The restaurant has two tables in the lower section and seven tables in the upper section. Antonio and Roberta, with the help of a chef, run the entire operation. All but one of the seven tables in our area were occupied by Americans. A table of six, from what we could overhear, were American restaurant owners and/or restaurant chefs who had come to have lunch and interact with Antonio. We had an excellent lunch, accompanied by a bottle of Brunello di Montalcino.

Our last day trip during this down time was to the town of Gubbio. From Perugia, you can drive northeast towards Ravenna and then go east through steep verdant mountains, then south to Gubbio. Or you can drive southeast from Perugia, then go east for a short while, and drive north through a long fertile agricultural valley to Gubbio. We took the mountainous road going and the valley road returning. Both were delightful drives.

Gubbio has an ancient history, as in centuries BC, and, like most Italian hilltop towns, or in this case a slope side town on Mount Ingino in the Apennine range, it spent a thousand years warring with surrounding towns. Gubbio has a Roman Theater in an open field outside the northwest side of the town, seating 16,000 spectators. Unfortunately, the theater, while visually impressive as you drive towards the town, is in such a state of disrepair that it is closed to visitors. Gubbio is also the town, as legend has it, where St. Francis tamed a wolf that had been attacking the town's farm animals.

Unlike the warm and welcoming ambiance that Assisi and Spello project due to the light color of the stone used in the construction of their buildings, many of the buildings in Gubbio were constructed with dark gray stone, giving the town an austere and foreboding look. The gothic architecture and medieval buildings don't add any warmth to the town's image. The town, however, is worth a visit: the people are delightful, the vistas are superb, especially from the Basilica of Saint Ubaldo on the top of Gubbio; and the restaurants, shops, and attractions are plentiful. We dined at Taverna Del Lupo, where the meal and service were excellent.

Soon we would drop Jack at his pensione for 10 days as we embarked on our next adventure to Rome, Muro Lucano, Potenza, and Sorrento. Unless the Italian bureaucracy struck again, we would return with two Apostille certified birth certificates and one Apostille certified marriage certificate. After our return, we had 10 days left in Italy and six days in Germany before we headed home.

Chapter Twenty-Two

Rome — Muro Lucano — Potenza — Sorrento

Sunday, October 7 to Friday October 26

Our decision as to when to spend time in Rome came late in our Italian adventure. When you plan only weeks in advance instead of many months in advance, securing decent accommodations in a city like Rome can be a challenge. After failing to find availability at two boutique hotels recommended by friends (Hotel Santa Maria and Hotel Campo de' Fiori,), we ended up making reservations at Hotel Palazzo Cardinal Cesi, which according to the hotel's website, was close to the Vatican.

The drive to the center of Rome, which I was dreading, turned out to be reasonably painless. Giselle got us to our hotel with little drama, perhaps because we entered the city on a Sunday afternoon in October. The hotel, which opens onto Via della Conciliazione, was indeed close to the Vatican, less than 100 yards from the entrance to St. Peter's Square, which really isn't a square at all. The building in which the hotel sits was both a former monastery and a former nunnery.

The hotel is square with a large sculpted interior garden that opens to the sky. The registration office, cocktail, and dining areas sit at the side opposite the front entrance. The hotel occupies 20 some rooms, and the rest of the building is used by members of a religious order. Every morning the staff slides a single sheet of paper under each door. The sheet does not contain the weather forecast or recommended tour activities. It contains three Bible passages suitable for the day ahead. And what else would you expect from a nunnery occupying a building named after a Cardinal?

If you exit the hotel front, take a few steps to your left and look straight across, down the street you can see a massive 25-foot tall fortress-type wall that runs all the way from the Vatican to the fortress, Castel Sant'Angelo, about half a mile away and the place where Tosca leapt to her death. Inside this massive wall is a not so secret passage that allowed the Pope to escape to the safety of the fortress any time Rome or the Vatican came under attack, which according to history, happened quite a few times.

Such an escape took place in 1527 when the mutinous army of the Roman Emperor sacked Rome because they had not been paid for their last battle campaign.

At that time, Cardinal Cesi, who lived in the building that was now our hotel, was the keeper of the Vatican treasury, some parts of which were stored in the vaults below the hotel. According to the hotel brochure, somehow, the good Cardinal was able to secure and move all the items of the treasury to Castel Sant'Angelo in the nick of time, thus becoming something of a hero within Vatican circles. And now, he has a hotel named after him.

— § —

This was our first visit to Rome. I can only echo what millions before me have said — it is a stunning city. If you can take one picture in Rome, you can take a million pictures in Rome. Just capturing on film the sculptured figures decorating bridges throughout the city could keep you busy for weeks. To do Rome right, we contracted with a gentleman named Nino, whose one-man company is called "Nino Knows." A fellow Cliffs member from the Cliffs at Keowee Falls recommended Nino, and we found that Nino, indeed, Knows Rome.

Monday afternoon, we spent four hours with Nino touring the Vatican museum, the Sistine Chapel, and St. Peter's Basilica. Tough to find all the right adjectives: amazing, striking, beautiful, jaw-dropping, unbelievable, incredible, and on and on. Tuesday afternoon, we did the hop-on and hop-off bus and wandered on our own. Wednesday afternoon, we met Nino for tours of Mussolini's headquarters, the National Monument to Vittorio Emanuele II, the Forum, Circus Maximus, and the Colosseum. Ditto on the adjectives.

I had visions that visiting Rome in October would be a delight, and the mild traffic we encountered on our drive to our hotel reinforced my visions. All of that changed when we went to the Vatican Museum. Despite our "skip the line" museum tickets, the crowds at the Vatican were stifling. More than 25,000 people a day now visit the Vatican Museum and Sistine Chapel. That's a 400 percent increase over the 5,000 people who used to visit the Vatican 10 to 12 years ago.

When you can't walk down a 200-yard-long and 15-yard-wide museum hallway because it is crammed with people, and you can move only when the folks in front of you move, it seriously detracts from the experience. The crowds in the Sistine Chapel were so dense that a person could have fainted but would have remained upright. Thank goodness, we had Nino along to guide, instruct, entertain, and distract us from the maddening crowd.

Having spent only three full days in Rome, I am now considerably more envious of Ed and Liz, our friends from the Cliffs at Keowee Springs. They spent nearly two months in Rome two years ago, when Ed taught business law as a visiting professor of Clemson University. We dined at two of Ed and Liz's favorite restaurants: Il Bacaro, our favorite of the two, and La Rosetta. We also dined at two of Chris and Dave's favorites: Lo Scopettaro and La Sagrestia, which was our favorite of those two.

— § —

Our hotel had an arrangement with a parking garage, so one of the garage's representatives picked up our car shortly after checking in and then delivered it back to us at 6:30 a.m. on Thursday, early enough for us to slip out of Rome before the morning rush hour began. The landscape between Rome and Naples is significantly different from Umbria and Tuscany. The land seems less devoted to agricultural pursuits than the other provinces, and the mountains appear stark and devoid of vegetation. Regardless, the drive was beautiful in its own right.

We arrived in Muro Lucano in time to park and locate the Comune office before it closed for the day at noon. Like Gubbio, Muro Lucano is a reasonably steep hillside town whose buildings are painted in beautiful but muted light pastel colors. Approaching the town by car is like approaching Positano or Amalfi by boat. You get the same pleasing landscape of colorful buildings stacked in layers, one higher but narrower than the other, cresting at the pinnacle of available land. The town sits at the foot of the Apennine mountains, and to its west side lies a narrow but fertile agricultural valley that runs north and south of the town.

After parking in the town square, we approached a small gathering of elderly residents as to the location of the Comune office and its records clerk, Antonietta Capezio. All the folks knew Antonietta, and why not – the town has a population of only slightly more than 5,000. More than 50 percent of this town's citizens are 40 years or older, so this old Italian town is not getting any younger any time soon.

The Comune office was a couple of short streets away, and Antonietta was there to greet us. She already had the three documents prepared and sitting in a folder on her desk. Kathy gave her passport to Antonietta, as well as the form that Maurizio prepared for her. A few administrative steps and 20 Euros later, we left the Comune di Muro Lucano with Kathy's great grandparents' birth records and their marriage record. Without these three documents, Kathy's quest for dual citizenship would have been dead in the water.

We toured the back streets of Muro Lucano for a while, mainly because we took a few wrong turns and couldn't figure how to extract ourselves from where we had driven. Giselle was of little help, but after some additional wrong turns and some extra correct turns, we were on our way to Potenza, the seat of the province, to have the Apostille certification added to our documents. Your guess is as good as ours as to why we could not get the Apostille done in Muro Lucano.

Potenza is the only hilltop town in Italy that we have not enjoyed. In fact, there was nothing about Potenza that we did enjoy. I would go further and say that Potenza is a town to be avoided at all costs. But we had no choice. It appeared that Potenza has more cars per capita and less parking spaces per capita than any town we have encountered. The streets are more twisted and narrower than any town we have encountered, and the drivers less friendly than any we have encountered.

We arrived in Potenza in time for lunch, and for the first time in Italy, we had a tough time finding a decent place to eat, and what we ended up with was not all that decent. Furthermore, the Prefettura, the office that affixes the Apostille certification, is in one of the Comune di Potenza offices at the top of the town, and parking spaces in the area are few and far between. Since we were supposed to arrive at the Prefettura's office at 5:00 p.m., we made several dry runs past the office to see what parking was like. The closest we came to a parking space was over five blocks away.

Trying to kill time in a town like Potenza is cruel and unusual punishment. Not being able to stand it anymore, at 3:40 p.m. we left our holding pattern and decided to head up to the Comune office and see what parking was like. Fortunately, we secured a parking space about two blocks from the office, and upon arrival by foot at the piazza, we entered a coffee shop to kill even more time. While Kathy enjoyed a cappuccino, I headed to the office building to make sure that it was the correct building to meet our needs.

With the help of the translation app, the police officer assured me that the building housed the Prefettura office, and that the office opened at 4:00. Even though our appointed time was 5:00, we took a chance and returned at 4:00, where the police officer escorted us to the office in question. Inside the office was one older, lovely lady who spoke no English. In anticipation of this eventuality, using the translation app, I had pre-scripted an explanation of why we were there and what we needed. The lady read the translation and then launched into an exhaustive speech of which we understood nothing.

I gave the time out sign, and then called Maurizio – it went to voice mail. One more time out sign, and then I called Giuseppe – success. After a many minute conversation, the lady handed me back the phone and Giuseppe proceeded to explain. Attaching the Apostille certifications to our three documents was not going to be a problem; however, the work could not be done that afternoon as promised. But if we came back at 11:30 a.m. the next day, the documents would be ready. The bureaucracy strikes again.

Based on our original timeline of leaving Potenza around 6:00 p.m., we had pre-booked and pre-paid for a hotel half way between Potenza and Sorrento in the town of Battipaglia, which would leave a drive of about an hour and 20 minutes the next day to our final destination of Sorrento. Off we went to Battipaglia, a town that is easily forgettable, and we returned to Potenza the next morning around 11:15. It was two hours of extra driving we could have easily done without.

Employing the often-used parking practice of many Italians, I pulled up next to the Comune office, made sure other cars could pass me, and put on my flashers. As long as you put on your flashers, you can park almost anywhere in Italy. Ten minutes later, Kathy emerged with her three documents, each carrying the Apostille stamp of the Prefettura of Potenza. Arrivederci Potenza!

— § —

The drive from Potenza to Salerno was generally stress free. The drive from Salerno to the outskirts of Sorrento was challenging. The drive through numerous small towns along the coast into Sorrento proper was as stressful a drive as we had encountered due to the density of the traffic, the narrowness of the roads, the plethora of tourist busses, and the swarm of motor scooter drivers, most of whom have perfected the dare devil art of lane splitting.

Our hotel for five nights, the Palazzo Jannuzzi Relais, recommended to us by Dave and Joan, sits right on the town's main square. The hotel is absolutely delightful, the staff were super friendly, the breakfast was amazing, and the location could not have been better. Through the hotel, we pre-booked a tour of and lunch at a lemon tree and olive grove farm, a boat trip to Capri, a tour of Pompeii, and a boat trip along the Amalfi coast to Positano and the town of Amalfi.

After all was said and done, our favorite towns from least favorite to most favorite were: Positano, Amalfi, Capri, and Sorrento. And Sorrento was the winner by a wide margin. The town's main area is relatively flat, making it easy to sightsee. It has two beautiful harbors, so boat excursions to other coastal areas are plentiful. The streets are quaint and loaded with shops. And the town has amazingly good restaurants, most of which specialize in fresh seafood.

For our five nights in Sorrento, we dined at: Fauno Bar, which has one of the most extensive menus we saw in our time in Italy; MoMo, a small restaurant on a quiet piazza; Il Buco, Sorrento's only Michelin rated restaurant; Bagni Delfino, on the wharf in Marina Grande; and Zi'Ntonio. Zi'Ntonio was quite average, and Il Buco, was overpriced for the small servings and de-constructed foods it served.

Bagni Delfino, a favorite of Dave and Joan's, was the best restaurant we visited. The avocado and shrimp salad was exquisite, and the grilled Branzino was outstanding. As an ACLU attorney with a weak heart, you may not want to dine here or stay at the Hotel Cardinal Cesi for that matter. Instead of a dish of mints by the cash register, the restaurant had a bowl medals of the Blessed Virgin Mary, which the register attendant and wife of one of the owners assured me had been blessed by a priest. Only in Italy. I took two medals.

— § —

Of all the places we visited on this short trip, I was most affected by our visit to Pompeii. For me, reading about "Roman Ruins" in high school was not an emotionally significant experience; walking the grounds of Pompeii, however, was a different story. I was struck by how large the city of Pompeii was in 79 A.D., a thriving commercial city of between 10,000 and 20,000 people, depending on whose historical perspective you read.

According to different estimates, in a brief 18-hour period, from 2,000 to 16,000 of the town's population died, and the city was completely covered in ash, a fact that slowly faded into history and was not brought back to the world's consciousness until 1748, when serious work began on excavating Pompeii's ruins. Most of those who died, died from inhaling the extremely hot gasses that enveloped the city. Others perished from the collapse of roofs that eventually failed under the pressure of thousands of pounds of volcanic ash.

The collective work of archeologists from the past 270 years in cleaning up and restoring Pompeii is remarkable. It's hard for me to comprehend the architectural and engineering talent it took to construct such a well-organized, yet compact city three to four centuries B.C. It was quite an experience to walk the streets of Pompeii and see in the stones below my feet the ruts that the commercial carts made more than 2,000 years ago. If interested in more, the YouTube video "Lost World of Pompeii (Ancient Rome Documentary) Timeline" does an excellent job describing what Pompeii was like in its heyday.

— § —

After 10 days at his pensione, Jack was happy to see us and vice versa. Despite his early skin issue, Jack adjusted really well to life in Italy, and why not; he was able to go everywhere, well almost everywhere, and everywhere he did go, people showered him with attention. Once we return to South Carolina, I can see therapy in Jack's future when he fails to be the center of attention as he was in Italy.

Returning Jack to South Carolina appeared to be less complicated than bringing him to Europe, mainly because all the vaccinations and shots he received six months ago were valid for a year. While no International Travel Certificate was required, we decided to get one for him anyway, just in case. Off to see Doctor Massimo one last time.

A final visit to Dr. Massimo was timely because I was worried about Jack's memory, vision, and hearing for the past few months. At Villa Nuba, with a treat in hand, when I signaled and said "sit," his butt was on the ground in a nanosecond. When I signaled and said "down," he was on the ground in a heartbeat. However, when we went to a restaurant, and I said "sit" and "down," he pretended not to hear me, repeatedly. When I did get eye contact with him and gave the commands, he looked at me like I was speaking a foreign language and proceeded to ignore me.

Turns out that Jack's memory and vision were fine. It had been two months or more since our last visit to Dr. Massimo. When we walked up to the outside door of the office, Jack was noticeably apprehensive. On previous visits, when we rang the doorbell, Massimo's wife opened the door and showed us into the waiting area. This time, Massimo opened the door and when Jack saw him, he bolted for the street, almost dislocating my shoulder.

When I finally got him into the waiting room, Jack sat and proceeded to tremble uncontrollably. I could do nothing to console him. When Massimo's wife appeared, Jack relaxed a bit. Jack survived the health exam, including use of the massive rectal thermometer, but when the door to the street opened, he wasted no time vacating the premises.

— § —

Our final excursion before leaving Italy involved going back to Montepulciano to meet Terry and Shellie, friends of ours from Cliffs at Keowee Falls. Both CPAs, but CPAs with personalities, Terry and Shellie own and operate an accounting firm in New Orleans. On a tour of Switzerland and Italy, their itinerary brought them to a former castle that is now a hotel near Montalcino. With Montepulciano about an hour drive from each of us, it was the perfect place to meet. We shared a fun few hours touring the city and ended with a superb lunch at Osteria Del Conte.

The next day, we would pull up stakes and head back to Germany for a short stay, and then fly back to the U.S.

PICTURES

PART II

Ditto

Civita di Bagnoregio – Feet don't fail me now!

Why does Guinness taste so much better in
Ireland?

Mission accomplished!

Maurizio Casalena, wife Monica, and daughter
Francesca

I am bored; want to play?

Will that be five gallons of white wine or red wine?

The main attraction – Branzino encrusted in salt at Osteria
Ae Botti, Giudecca, Venice

Early dinner with Lorena at La Sagrestia Ristorante in Rome

The hillside village of Muro Lucano, province of Potenza, in the region of Basilicata, Italy

Goodbye to Giselle II after 10,951 kilometers

Jack's travel crate. So far, he has been in two continents, three European countries, three German cities, 17 Italian cities, and nine U.S. states.

Chapter Twenty-Three

Final Thoughts

Saturday, October 27 to Saturday, November 3

After six months, my Italian was flowing effortlessly from my lips, with perfect pronunciation, and with proper situational accuracy. The only problem was that we were now in Germany. Having lived in Germany for three and a half years, I am good at survival German. It's just every time I tried to speak German during this short stay, Italian words popped out. There must have been a short circuit somewhere in my brain.

The really good news about being in Germany, other than the beer, scenery, and food, was that I couldn't be arrested for driving in Italy without an Italian driving permit. Which was something I was not aware I needed, and which must be obtained before you enter Italy, because once you are in Italy, you can't apply for one. Seems kind of silly, no?

Our three days in Garmisch were delightful, although the cool temperatures, mainly in the 30s, were a little shock to our respective systems, with Jack apparently the least affected of the three of us. Our three days at the Munich Airport Hilton were relaxing and allowed us time to contemplate how to put 80 pounds of stuff in a 70-pound suitcase, an exercise we repeated four times over.

We bade farewell to Giselle II, who was as amazing as Giselle I. With Giselle I, we logged 4,488 kilometers; with Giselle II, we logged 10,951 kilometers for a total of 15,439 kilometers, or approximately 9,264 miles. No tickets issued, which could have been problematic; no involvement in any accidents, which could have been disastrous; and no dents, dings, or scratches caused by me.

Jack was another story. On one of our trips to the pensione, I made the mistake of rolling the rear window all the way down and Jack got so excited to be at the kennel that he tried to climb out the window, putting hundreds of small scratches in the top third of the door. Scratch remover, rubbing compound, and elbow grease remedied the damage to the point it was barely noticeable even to me, because I knew where to look, and, thankfully, not noticeable to the inspector at the car lease agency when I returned the car. I had full comprehensive insurance, so damage of any kind was not a real concern.

Racking up 10,000 steps a day on those days that we ventured out from Villa Nuba was never an issue – 14,000 to 16,000 steps a day was common, and the majority of those steps involved elevation of some degree. Knowing we would do a lot of walking, I purchased two pair of Merrell pull-on walking/hiking shoes. Not having owned Merrell shoes before, I was hopeful they would do the trick. Turns out they were amazing: durable, very sturdy over uneven surfaces, and extremely comfortable. And, unlike the rest of my clothes, six months later, the shoes still fit.

If a lady can sue McDonalds because the coffee that she spilled in her lap was too hot, then I should be able to sue Italy for unintended weight gain. Who knew that eating pasta and drinking wine every day could lead to significant weight gain? There were no warning labels in any restaurant or on anything we ate or drank. I think we have a case. Then there is the carpel tunnel in my right wrist from twisting pasta each day for six months. A double lawsuit, perhaps.

Given the multitude of towns and cities we dined in, slept in, or toured, we never felt threatened at any time night or day. No one ever accosted us, or hassled us, or looked cross at us, or stole from us, or picked our pockets, or broke into our car. The only times I felt in danger for my life were the times Lorena Bobbitt-Houlihan made an appearance.

The check-in process to return home from Munich was reasonably uncomplicated for Kathy and me. For Jack, it was the mirror image of the inbound flight. No one was interested in the reams of paperwork pertaining to Jack, and once his crate was inspected, a baggage handler whisked him away to await loading.

When we came through Munich passport control, upon reviewing our two U.S. passports, the German customs officer's demeanor turned grim, and he questioned the fact that we had stayed in the European Union for over 90 days. When I presented my EU Passport and explained we were married, he waved us through and wished us safe travels. Were all those trips with Giuseppe to Perugia's bureaucratic maze for naught?

Once onboard, I was awash in guilt for what we had put Jack Daniels through. So, I assuaged my guilt with some Jack Daniel's on the rocks. As we hoped it would be, the return flight was uneventful. After 13 hours in his crate, Jack appeared a little disoriented, but once we reached a spot where he could relieve himself, his disposition started improving.

While we had to go through a secondary customs screening because we were bringing in a live animal, no one looked at any documentation. When I replied in the affirmative to the question, "Has your dog had a rabies shot within the past 12 months?" the customs officer waved us through to our awaiting driver.

Home now for a few months, as I reflect on our experience of living in Italy, it all seems surreal. Every now and then, when recounting our adventures, I shake my head and mumble that I can't believe we undertook such a crazy adventure and brought our dog along for the ride. Am I pleased we made the trip? Absolutely. Knowing what I know now, would I do it again? Perhaps not with a four-legged family member. But ignorance is bliss, and all things considered, having Jack along enriched the experience in ways we could not have anticipated. That said, if I have a Lorena-like really bad day, who knows where we might end up.

Living in Italy for the six months did disabuse Kathy of the notion of permanently living there. Despite the pace of life, and the wonderful sights, and the delicious food, and the inexpensive wines, we are happy to be home. Regardless, we are going forward with Kathy's Italian Passport application so that if we decide to undertake a similar but shorter adventure to her homeland, we will be prepared.

I still keep in touch with Giuseppe and Maurizio on a regular basis, and I suspect in the coming years we will see one or both of them here in South Carolina. Reliving our adventures in person with them would call for opening the really good Brunello.

A couple of months back, I received an email from Giuseppe about the fact that he had recently bumped into a friend of his who works at the Polizia Nazionale, to whom he relayed in excruciating detail the saga we experienced in trying to get a Carta di Soggiorno for Kathy.

According to Giuseppe, this gentleman stated that we just need to write him an email, in Italian, of course, outlining a series of data points he requested, with supporting documentation, and he would take care of issuing the residency card.

Giuseppe, you can't be serious!

Acknowledgments

To my wife, Kathy, for being such a trooper on our six-month Italian adventure and for having such a great sense of humor. Perhaps more importantly, for being willing to accept my warped sense of humor.

To Jennifer Houlihan, my nephew Philip's wife, for being willing to act as my editor and for taking my weekly email blog postings about this adventure and molding them into something infinitely more readable.

To Dave and Joan Parsons, who recommended staying at Villa Nuba, our apartment in Perugia, and for their priceless advice on places to visit and things to do throughout Italy.

To Giuseppe Nuzzaci, our landlord at Villa Nuba and host in Perugia, for going above and beyond in helping us acclimate to our Italian surroundings and helping us navigate the Italian bureaucracy.

To Dr. Massimo Crecco and his wife, Simona, for taking such great care of Jack Daniels when he was having some difficult-to-diagnose health issues.

To Josie, Nicoletta, and chef Claudio Brugalossi, at La Taverna Ristorante, for making all of us feel so welcome every time we dined with them.

To Flavia and Matteo Ferracci and their assistant, Ilaria, at the Parco Cinofilo Umbro dog pensione in Perugia for taking such good care of Jack Daniels while we were travelling outside Perugia.

To Noel McCarthy for going out of his way to help us, complete strangers, research my wife's Italian ancestry.

To Maurizio Casalena whose tireless efforts on our behalf allowed us to fill in the blanks on Kathy's Italian ancestry and helped us gain access to the records we needed to complete Kathy's passport application.

ABOUT THE AUTHOR

Dan Houlihan was born in Mountmellick, Ireland, and later lived in Mullingar, Ireland, until he was 11 years old, at which time he emigrated to Omaha, Nebraska, with his mother and four of his seven siblings. Dan has an undergraduate degree from Creighton University and a graduate degree from Florida Institute of Technology. After a 20-year career as an Army officer, Dan served in several information technology positions with the State of Indiana, ending as Chief Information Officer. He then became CEO of two subsidiaries of the e-government technology company, NIC, Inc. Dan has a daughter, Tracie, and two grandchildren living in Portland, Oregon. Now retired, Dan and his wife Kathy and their Labrador Retriever, Jack Daniels, reside in the Cliffs at Keowee Springs in Six Mile, South Carolina. Dan enjoys golf, travel, skiing, good company, good food, and good wine.

Questions or comments can be sent to JacksItalianAdventure@gmail.com.

ABOUT THE EDITOR

Jennifer Cox Houlihan is the author of *Triumphant Womanhood: God's Never "Whatever."* She has a degree in journalism from the University of North Carolina at Chapel Hill. Jennifer is a homeschool teacher, a lifestyle model, and is the director of Peachtree Arts Academy, a non-profit organization devoted to music education. She and her husband, a commercial airline pilot, have five children and live in Georgia. Find her at Facebook.com/JenniferHoulihanTriumphant or Instagram @jenhoulihan.

Made in the USA
Columbia, SC
22 February 2020